D1392943

UP AND OVER

For my dad, Stan Hadfield,
and my granddaughters,
Freya and Marnie Linahan.

UP AND

A Trek Through Rugby League Land

OVER

Dave Hadfield

MAINSTREAM
PUBLISHING

EDINBURGH AND LONDON

First published in Great Britain in 2004 by
MAINSTREAM PUBLISHING COMPANY (EDINBURGH) LTD
7 Albany Street
Edinburgh EH1 3UG

Reprinted 2004

ISBN 1 84018 818 9

A catalogue record for this book is available from the British Library

Typeset in Apollo, Baskerville MT and Frutiger

Printed in Great Britain by
Mackays of Chatham plc

Contents

Introduction

THE M62 CORRIDOR GETS A BAD PRESS. I SHOULD KNOW; I
give it one. Like most people involved in rugby league, I have a
love–hate relationship with that ribbon of tarmac which largely
defines its scope.

During the course of 2003, I watched matches in Cumbria,
Scotland, Wales, London and points between, but the vast majority
took place somewhere along that slender slice of the north of
England between Hull and Widnes.

It is the compact geography of rugby league that makes it possible
to flit to and fro between these poles on its axis. It is the
concentrated pattern of local rivalries along the way that gives the
game much of its passion and vitality.

And yet it can also feel like a prison – an infuriatingly limiting
regime, beyond which the sport is doomed to struggle in vain for
the same sense of belonging. You don't have to go very far from the
M62 – Sheffield or Chorley, for instance – to feel that, despite the
presence of professional teams, you have wandered away from the
mainstream.

There has been a broadening of horizons over the last couple of
decades, less through the cautious, one-step-forward-one-step-back
expansion of the professional game than through the genuinely
nationwide RL Conference, through the students and the armed forces.

Rugby league has a foothold in all sorts of apparently unlikely places, but to get within a long touch-finder of everywhere – apart from London – where it is played at top level, you only need to go down one road, between Junctions 7 and 38. Small wonder we sometimes suffer from claustrophobia.

* * *

On the other hand, when you think of walking across England, Hull and Widnes are hardly the starting and finishing points you would instinctively mark down.

I imagined myself following in my dad's footsteps, perhaps, on the classic Coast to Coast route from St Bees Head to Robin Hood's Bay. Or maybe, as I did in 2002, walking Hadrian's Wall from Carlisle to Newcastle – almost a rugby league route if you divert to Gateshead, but a bit thin on obvious connections in the middle section.

True, there is a relatively new Trans Pennine Trail, snaking its way from Hull to Liverpool, through South Yorkshire and the southern fringes of Manchester, but I don't think I would ever have tackled that.

Last spring, though, I heard on the grapevine that there was a plan taking shape for a trek from the Humber to the Mersey, taking in all the Super League grounds and raising money for the Outward Bound Trust along the way.

As good causes go, Outward Bound sounded fine; it takes young people out of some pretty disadvantaged circumstances and shows them the possibilities of outdoor adventure – often with life-changing results. But my motivation was more selfish; it seemed like an unrepeatable opportunity to see Rugby League Land in a new way.

I would be going through all the places that were deeply familiar to me from years of watching matches there, of going there to talk to players, coaches and other people involved in the game. But this would take me through at walking pace, seeing places from different angles and possibly getting a sense of the elements that bind all these towns together, as well as the fiercely observed distinctions that keep them apart. After all, people from a little way further south in England can't tell any of us apart, yet we have all these tiny gradations between native and alien upon which we rely for our identities. It might also be an excuse for a 220-mile pub crawl.

It's a long way, 220 miles, so you had better pick your companions carefully. As a latecomer to the project, I had no choice in the matter; the rest of the team was signed up and I was merely the eve-of-deadline recruit that might just give the finishing touch to the line-up, or might bugger it up completely.

The architects of the whole thing were the Clarke brothers – the former Great Britain loose forward (and current team manager) and Sky TV touchline presence, Phil, and his brother, Andy – who, if anything, has a finger in even more rugby league pies.

We go back a fair distance. I remembered their dad, Colin, as a Wigan coach and, before that, their hooker; in fact, Phil once set me a real poser by asking me: 'Was my dad a dirty player?'

'Well, put it this way,' I said, after due deliberation. 'He wasn't the dirtiest hooker around. He wasn't the dirtiest hooker called Clarke. In fact, he wasn't even the second dirtiest hooker called Clarke. But, yes, he was still pretty bad.'

What's more, their mum taught my youngest daughter – and never stiff-armed her or late-tackled her once.

One of the Clarke family's characteristics is an enviable ability to keep 20 balls in the air at the same time. They call it multi-tasking these days, I believe, but it means they've always got several things on the go. I'd been involved in one of them and it made me wonder whether I was really the sort of person they wanted to have around for 220 miles.

Rugbee.com was part of the internet boom, at a time when it looked as though there were millions to be made from the world wide web, as opposed to the millions which have been sunk into it without trace.

I should have known from the start that it was too high-tech for me and too much like real work, compared with what I do most of the time. The clue was in the lavishly illustrated section that was intended to introduce us to the waiting world. The Clarkes – and everyone else they'd hired – were there in crisp collars and ties, clean-cut, bright-eyed and obviously eager to get to grips with the cutting edges of technology. And there was me – Hawaiian shirt, unruly beard, ill-gotten tan and equally ill-gotten beer-gut.

It looked like a gang of Mormon missionaries and someone they'd dragged out of a beach bar in Cairns. It looked like a mismatch that would end in a messy divorce – and it did.

Still, you shouldn't let ancient history get in the way of something you really want to do. Besides, *Rugbee.com* hadn't been all bad. It had provided another daughter with her first taste of paid employment, dressed up as a bee, handing out leaflets at a Test match at the Reebok Stadium. I just worry for her that it might all be downhill after a start like that.

So, if I hadn't been much of a worker, I might prove that I had a bit of worth as a walker. The one we were worried about was Mike Stephenson.

Stevo – even his wife and kids call him that – had finished his playing career 25 years earlier as something of a physical wreck. That's true of a lot of players, but not many of them play most of their career in a corset. Apart from the back, both his knees were pretty much gone and he was not, by his own admission, much of an enthusiast for exercise.

That led many to assume that he would pack it in after a few miles and probably spend the rest of the fortnight riding in one of the support vehicles, drinking champagne and eating foie gras. The funds of the Outward Bound Trust have been swelled considerably by those who laid money on Stevo not being able to last the distance.

After 'How are your feet?' the question I was most frequently asked after completing the Trek was 'How did you cope with Stevo for 220 miles?' Well, it was an experience – one which I can only compare with being handcuffed to the hyperactive boy on the school trip.

It wasn't that I didn't know what to expect. I could look back with affection to going with him to see his mum and dad in Dewsbury during a Kangaroo tour, not to mention an inebriated boat trip on the Hawkesbury in Sydney, which ended with an impromptu Australia versus England cricket match in a riverside clearing and nearly with arrest by the park rangers.

Since then, however, Stevo has become a Personality, with a capital P; an illuminated capital P, in the world of rugby league. The persona he has cultivated dominates Sky's coverage of the sport, so much so that his pronouncements often seem to be more important than the game itself to a lot of people. His face is better known than that of any player and even people who think they loathe the sight and sound of him find, when they meet him, that they love him really.

Life on the road with him was exhilarating, exasperating and exhausting, often all at the same time. It left me incurably fond of the old buffoon.

Neither he nor I could have got anywhere near the finishing line in Widnes, however, without the help of a remarkable support team. One thing that kept me going was the thought that, if I stopped, I would have to take on all the myriad duties that they performed to keep Phil, Stevo and me on the move. If it comes to a choice between pain and work – proper, organisational work – give me pain any time.

The route was planned by Andy and his and Phil's uncle, Bernard Lundy. He was a rugby union wing-forward for Orrell for the best part of 20 years – which still makes him something of a renegade in the Clarke–Lundy clan – and is still enviably fit. He could have walked the whole route with ease, but instead contented himself with looking after the three of us like a mother hen, keeping us clear of oncoming traffic, slowing us down, speeding us up and generally ensuring that we got to where we were meant to be.

Like any decent team, we also had strength in depth. There was Nina, a recent graduate in politics from Hull University and a formidable prop forward for the women students' international side. She passed up the chance of a playing trip to Moscow to be part of the Trek and was a tower of strength throughout, particulary when binding up Stevo's suppurating feet before each day's march – scenes reminiscent of a biblical leper colony.

There were Marie and Adam, students from St Helens and surely destined to be the Posh and Becks of their generation. There was Phil, our semi-official photographer from Belfast, and his wife, Gill, who looked at times as though she was pondering divorcing him for persuading her to spend part of her teacher's holiday pounding the tarmac in East Yorkshire and running errands for a bunch of overgrown kids. They were replaced, in a complicated pattern of rolling substitutions, by Roy and Peter, who, with his master's degree from Oxford, was probably the most over-qualified of the lot of us.

It was the sort of squad that you look at before the start of the season and think: 'We might go OK here.' Messrs Clarke and Stephenson reckoned that the *esprit de corps* was the closest thing they had experienced to a Great Britain tour. It wasn't quite like any tour I've been on – nobody was sent home in disgrace or abandoned without trace behind enemy lines – but I knew what they meant.

I was hugely dependent on the efficiency of the back-up team, because I was not only trying to walk 220 miles, I was also trying to keep notes. I had even attempted to go high-tech and belatedly enter the twenty-first century, but despaired of my Dictaphone – borrowed from my mate Keith's desk at Bolton Housing Department – when I failed to record Nick Barmby intelligibly before setting out from Hull. You wouldn't believe, either, how hard it is to handle a pencil and notebook on the move without doing yourself a serious injury.

I was also under the misapprehension that there would be time, during and after the days' walking, to wander off on little side-trips to see people and places I wanted to get into this book. The reality was rather different. Obergruppenführer Clarke described the pace required as being like 'crossing a car park in the rain' and, by the end of 18 miles of that, all you wanted to do was to collapse into a sauna or steam-room, swimming pool or – best of all – a jacuzzi, before going out to sing for your supper at some rugby league ground or other.

That is why I've had to go back to a few places en route to which I wasn't able to devote time. It's cheating, but what the heck. Even more impressively, I actually did a bit of advance research in one or two places, so some of the material from those visits also appears in this book. If you had us bugged every step of the way and you don't remember a few of the encounters I'm about to relate, there's your reason.

There are also a few hiccups in the continuity, because there were occasions when we were staying overnight and/or appearing at various fans' forums on a completely different day than the one on which we walked through that town. Rather than take you on a zig-zag journey back and to across the north of England that would leave both you and me exhausted and disorientated, I've occasionally rearranged things according to where they happened, rather than necessarily when. It's like being God, really.

If that sounds a bit of a scam, I can reassure you of one thing. We managed the whole trek, even Stevo – although there were times when we all wished he would subside gently on his bloodied stumps and give us a bit of peace.

As well as irritation, though, Stevo provided plenty of inspiration. My thanks go to him and the rest of the party for making possible such a memorable experience, to the hotels which put us up for free or for very little, to the individuals and businesses which fed and watered us, to the clubs which organised fund-raising efforts on our behalf, to Sky Sports for their active involvement and help, to the firms which provided all manner of outdoor gear for our use and abuse and to the hundreds – nay thousands – of people who joined us for part of the route. One of the attractions of the idea was that it would be a celebration of the diverse and sometimes dysfunctional family of rugby league and that was the way it worked out.

On a personal level, I owe a debt to my own family for putting up with another disrupted summer. I feel especially bad for not spending more time with my wonderful granddaughters, Freya and Marnie. I must acknowledge that it is the influence of my dad, Stan Hadfield, still striding out at the age of 88 as this book is published, that has turned me into a compulsive walker who would see nothing wrong in going out and doing this sort of thing. So blame your great-grandad, girls.

My friends, Keith Fenton and Mike Latham, provided invaluable help with logistics and transport and I must also thank all the other friends and acquaintances who gave me the extra motivation to stay the course by sponsoring me. *The Independent* helped as well, by giving me licence to work in an even more ramshackle way than usual for the duration of the walk. It turned out to be a nice, quiet fortnight to be away from the desk, with only a couple of coaching casualties, a few drugs revelations, three players going to prison, and another losing a leg. The way this news filtered through and the various reactions to it gave the fortnight another running storyline.

I must make a special mention of a neighbour I only know as Dave the Hypnotist, who shoved a £50 note in my hand at the bowling club soon after the walk. Apart from the hypnotic practice he runs, curing people of sporting injuries by putting them under the influence, he has a second, messier job, cleaning up scenes of crimes and infested council houses. I can't see for the life of me why he doesn't combine the two by hypnotising people and sending them out to do the dirty work. That is exactly the sort of question that can occur to you when you find yourself somewhere in the north of England, between Hull and Widnes, between agony and ecstasy, shadowing that damned M62 through Rugby League Land. Enjoy the journey with me.

I

Hull: Almost Like Being Abroad

THERE WAS A BRIEF TIME, AT THE START OF THE '80S, WHEN I seriously considered doing something that few people from west of the Pennines do. I thought about moving to Hull, but wasn't sure that I was ready to live abroad again.

Things are subtly different there. They have 'fern' boxes, which I first assumed to be something to do with the Britain in Bloom contests, but which turn out to be what the rest of us call phone boxes. Those phone boxes are creamy white, because Kingston upon Hull, to give it its Sunday name, ran its own system in splendid isolation when the rest of the country had all been lumped in together. It has a station called Paragon, whatever that is all about. 'These people are pleasant but queer,' wrote J.B. Priestley in his *English Journey* in 1933. 'They are queer because they are not quite Yorkshire but not quite anything else.'

The architecture often has more in common with Holland, Scandinavia and the Baltic than with Leeds or Bradford. For most of its history, you would be more likely to bump into a Russian or a Swede in the city centre — and certainly around the docks — than you would a Lancastrian. Even the new KC Stadium — brought to you by the good folk who kept the phone boxes white — has a continental feel, set as it is in the middle of parkland.

Back in the early '80s, Humberside — by which I mean the area, rather than the ill-fated, unloved county that dared not speak its name – was the centre of the rugby league universe. Australian crowds were in a slump, the Wigan boom had not begun and, for a short time, Hull FC were the best-supported team in the world. With their galaxy of imported stars – from New Zealand as well as from their more traditional hunting grounds in the West Riding – they were certainly the most glamorous, with Hull Kingston Rovers, similarly bolstered by big-name Kiwis, not that far behind. Then there was another kind of glamour, in the shape of the women – the toughest-looking women I'd ever seen – who made up a good part of their support. There was a sort of uniform; spray-on ice-blue jeans with white stilettos for Hull, the same with red for Rovers. Trying to see all the big matches at that time, I found myself coming to Hull every other week. It seemed sensible for a while to just up sticks and live there, but the moment passed.

Even now, though, a trip to Hull always seems to me like a foreign holiday for which you don't need a passport. It is a place of culture, of the poetry of Andrew Marvell and of Philip Larkin, author of that most soothing of bedtime rhymes: 'They tuck you up, your mum and dad . . .' There is the legacy of William Wilberforce and the abolition of slavery, as well as the pub, the Old White Hart, where the Civil War was brought closer by the decision to bar Charles I from the town. It even has, just around the corner from there, a street called The Land of Green Ginger – a name too whimsical even for a self-respecting theme park but one oddly at home in Hull.

There is also – inevitably, you might feel by the end of our route – a museum devoted to what used to be the dominant industry. The Hull Maritime Museum celebrates the fishing that sustained the area for centuries. Opposing fans still chant 'You Only Sing When You're Fishing' – surely one of the more amiable insults in the national repertoire – and Hull people routinely refer to themselves as codheads, but both are desperately out of date.

It throws them into a bit of confusion at the Maritime Museum when I ask them for information on the current state of the fishing industry.

'You're a bit late,' they say, by which they don't mean that they're about to close for the day.

'Ray, there's a chap here wants to know about the fishing nowadays.'

'There is none,' he says, coming down the central staircase of what used to be the Dock Offices.

He is only exaggerating slightly; there are, he says, only five trawlers operating out of Hull now, compared with the 365 – neat to have one for every day of the year – that constituted its high-water mark. In what seems almost like a calculated insult, most of the fish sold in Hull chippies is flown in from Iceland – clearly the victor in the Cod Wars – to Humberside Airport.

Like most things over which we now wax nostalgic, fishing was often a grim affair. Alongside the mighty displays of harpoons – because whaling was also big business here – the museum is full of accounts of men and boats lost at sea. 'The death toll in the fishing industry was the highest for that of any occupation', a print-out notes with something close to pride. Match that down your namby-pamby coal mines.

Near The Boulevard, the once elegant thoroughfare that leads past Hull's old ground, there is a memorial to the lives lost – those of the skipper, George Henry Smith, and the third hand, William Richard Leggett – when the trawler *Crane* was fired upon by the Russian Baltic Fleet in 1904, on the rather flimsy pretext that they thought it was a Japanese warship, during the war between those two countries. A footnote on the memorial also commemorates Walter Whelpton, skipper of the *Mino*, who 'died of shock' five months later, although presumably not at hearing the news of the *Crane*. Then there was the *Gaul*, lost with its crew in 1974 amid accusations, which still reverberate, that the Soviets were responsible and that there might have been a British spy on board. The relatives of those who perished have been represented, in their battle for a full enquiry, by a former Hull KR director, Max Gold. You are never very far from rugby league in anything that happens in Hull, or even in icy waters hundreds of miles away.

These incidents rankled rather more than the average acts of God and weather that took most lives, but all seemed to have been forgiven by the time a local amateur side, Embassy, became the first to host a Russian team, Strella Kazan, in the Challenge Cup in

December 2002. After that match, at Hull KRs' Craven Park, each Russian player was given an envelope containing a £10 note with which to start the evening's drinking. It has always seemed to me a generous city.

Traditionally, it is Hull FC that has the links with the fishing industry, with Rovers more closely allied with the freight docks. That means that Hull must have been watched by many of the breed immortalised in the song by Mike Waterson – one of the singing family from Hull – as 'Three Day Millionaires'. That was what they used to call the trawlermen on shore-leave, spending what must have seemed fat wage packets before going to sea again. 'I left school Friday and I started work on Saturday,' says the young trawlerman in the song.

> I'll get a deckie learning
> It's the bonus I'll be earning
> And the money it comes in handy for the old ran-tan
> Brylcreem in me hair
> Three Day Millionaire
> I couldn't give a bugger, I'm a man.

Terry Walker remembers the Three Day Millionaires, with their philosophy described in the sleeve notes of the Watersons' 1975 *Topic* LP as 'Work like horses, spend like asses', well enough. His grandad's job, after he stopped going to sea himself, was as a ship's runner, going from house to house rousing the crew from their post-binge stupor so that the trawlers could head for the fishing grounds again. When his grandad did go to sea, his grandma would never wash the pots while he was away – not because she was bone idle but because it was considered unlucky.

Terry never went out with the trawlers, but he is a hero of a different kind. If you've been to matches at The Boulevard or the KC Stadium over the last few years, you will have seen him, pushing his 14-year-old son, Scott, in a wheelchair. Scott has cerebral palsy, but such is his determination to be involved in everything rugby league, that, of everyone who was invited to the start of the Trek outside The Deep, Hull's swanky new museum of the oceans, thrusting out into the Humber like the prow of a huge glass ship, he was the one guaranteed to be there. He even referees matches with his dad carrying him on his back. These are not people easily beaten down.

The Deep is part of a wholesale gentrification of Hull's city centre waterfront. Like cities all over the world, it has transformed dockside dereliction into a selling point. From a hotel overlooking the marina, you feel closer to the North Sea trade routes than to the M62; even more so, as you watch the sun go down from outside the Minerva Hotel, famed for its giant haddock. (This is a city of superlatives: Britain's biggest Chinese restaurant; Europe's biggest council estate and biggest travelling fair; *Guinness Book of Records*-sized haddock, even if they are probably flown in by jumbo jet from Reykjavik.)

Wandering back to the Holiday Inn, however, with Nina waxing nostalgic about her remarkable record of breaking opposition collar-bones, no sooner has a phrase like 'I bet it used to be rough as boots down here' sneaked out than all hell breaks loose. Fifty yards away, mercifully separated from us by one of the network of docks, a full-scale battle erupts. The effect from that distance is like watching a wide-screen film – some local remake of *Gangs of New York* perhaps. Visually stunning against the last of the light in the sky, but I was happy to be where I was, rather than with a couple of other members of the party, right in the middle of it, crouching down behind some railings as the charge swept past. It was, apparently, locals versus Iranians, with one serious stabbing, 20 arrests and court cases pending. The process of gentrification is not quite complete on the dockside.

* * *

With the sun glinting on the Humber at the confluence with the River Hull – the traditional dividing line between Hull FC and KR territory – it is easy to believe in Hull as a successfully reinvented city, even if that East Hull–West Hull rivalry is as full of old-fashioned bitterness as any in the game. It spawned the charming ditty 'We're black, we're white, we'll never merge with shite,' when some fantasist suggested pooling their resources, and really hard-core Hull FC fans won't eat bacon, because it's red and white.

The crowds are gathering to get into The Deep, but also to see the Trek start or even to walk with us. There are some familiar faces among them. Nicky Barmby has played football for Spurs, Middlesbrough, Everton, Liverpool and Leeds, as well as 23 times for England, but he is Hull-born and bred and a rugby league lad at heart. He grew up on the terraces at The Boulevard and wanted to be Peter Sterling. Even now, he phones up Shaun McRae, the Hull coach, for regular chats about the team and its tactics and he gets to games whenever he can. He is there at the starting line to provide encouragement and guarantee extra publicity and he has a well-rehearsed little hymn of praise to rugby league and how football could learn a lot from its camaraderie and the ability of its players to knock seven colours out of each other and then share a couple of pints afterwards. 'In football, the egos have taken over,' he says. All perfectly true, but I can't help noticing that he's wearing flip-flops, which raises some questions about how far down the road he intends carrying his enthusiasm for the game of his youth. Still, it is probably only in Hull that you would find a footballer who has won 23 England caps and earned several times more money than a rugby league player could ever dream of, but who still not so secretly dreams of playing scrum-half in the irregular black and white hoops.

* * *

It is probably only in Hull, as well, that, if you had an empty theatre to fill, the sure-fire way of doing so would be to put on a play about rugby league. That's what John Godber did and the rest, as they say, is history. Godber comes from Upton, on the road between Wakefield and Doncaster, but in Castleford territory for spectating purposes. He really warmed to the game as a student in Leeds, however, watching Syd Hynes and Co. in the team of the early '70s. When he arrived in Hull, as artistic director of the Hull Truck Theatre Company, the Humberside rugby league boom was in full swing and he made a connection that changed everything, for him and the theatre.

'I had a theatre nobody was coming to, so I thought "Why not write a play about rugby league?"' That was the birth of *Up 'n' Under*, the play that transformed Hull Truck's fortunes and set up Godber as one of Britain's most-performed writers. The title is worth dwelling upon; it was the most durable of Eddie Waring's catchphrases, one that is still trotted out in the standard caricature of the northern, rugby league man's mode of speech. I could be quite sniffy about it, if I hadn't purloined it, spun it around and stuck it on the jacket of this book. Thanks for the loan, gentlemen.

Up 'n' Under was not the first play about rugby league. Godber acknowledges his debt to David Storey, who, apart from *This Sporting Life*, wrote a play called *The Changing Room*, which anticipates *Up 'n' Under* in many ways. But Godber's piece was a massive popular success, not only putting Hull Truck on the map, but also doing the rounds of audiences with no knowledge of or interest in the game. I remember seeing it staged in Shrewsbury and marvelling at how well it worked – particularly, and most surprisingly, the action sequences. Godber constructed those sections as an elaborately choreographed dance and was reassured that he had got it right by no less an authority than James Leuluai, one of Hull's famous Kiwis, who lived a couple of doors away.

Godber couldn't join us for the start of the Trek, because he was going on holiday that day. It was just as well, in one sense, because it's hard to look a man in the eye when he's taken the trouble to turn up and shed a little sweat and ask him: 'Why was the film so crap then?' Over the phone, I work around to it a bit more tactfully.

The answer, as with so many things in life, comes down to timing. Godber wanted to make the film as soon as he wrote it. 'But it took 17 years to get the funding. If it had been about rugby union, we'd have raised it in two phone calls. That says something about the attitude to rugby league: if it comes from the people, it can't be any good.'

The long delay in getting *Up 'n' Under* onto film meant that its potential audience was already suffering from Northern Humour Fatigue, thanks to the success of films like *The Full Monty* and *Brassed Off*. It also finished up being filmed in South Wales, which robbed it of any authentic sense of place, and was acted by a cast with little feel for the subject matter – my opinion, not Godber's, and with the former Halifax and St Helens prop Adam Fogerty and the dying Brian Glover excepted. 'If I'd had my way, they'd have all come from Upton,' he says. It shows that a man from Castleford's backyard, who lives in Hull, but somehow contrives to support Leeds, of all teams, hasn't entirely lost the script.

* * *

If Mr Godber is off on his holidays and Mr Barmby looks like he is ready for his, you can't knock the preparedness of Johnny Whiteley. The former Hull and Great Britain loose-forward was 72 at the time of the Trek, but he still had the enthusiasm of a young kid getting ready for his first game.

Not everyone who would like to join us is able to do so quite so effortlessly. Bobby Hutton, who broke his neck at the start of the season playing for the South London Storm, is at home in Hull from Pinderfields Hospital in Wakefield and now mobile enough to see us off. Phil Clarke's career was ended by a similar injury and he has kept in touch during his convalescence. You couldn't really have a better mentor.

Nor, walking through the otherwise deserted Sunday streets of Hull, could you have a better companion than Gentleman John Whiteley. That tag stuck with him throughout his career, which was famous for its untarnished aura of fair play as well as for its outstanding success. Mind you, you look at some of the other names in the Hull pack of the 1950s – Tommy Harris, the Drake twins – and they could probably afford one gentleman, much as Hull KR could with a similarly clean-cut player like Phil Lowe in a later era. In over 700 games as an amateur and a professional, Whiteley was never sent off.

'I should have been once or twice,' he admits. A case of giving a dog a good name, perhaps, but Whiteley remembers one particular match when he acted wildly out of character. It was a Yorkshire Cup final and one of the first matches to be televised by the BBC, with Eddie Waring – yes, him again – commentating. Only the second half was being screened and what the viewers hadn't seen was the opposing hooker clattering Johnny repeatedly in the first.

'And here come Hull, led back out by Johnny Whiteley,' said Waring. 'Gentleman Johnny Whiteley, the first gentleman of rugby league.' His first gentlemanly act of the second half was to exact overdue retribution by laying out the hooker.

'Bloody hell,' said the producer, fresh up from London and watching his first game of rugby league. 'If he's the gentleman, I can't wait for the hooligans to arrive.'

Whiteley was also a coach of note, being remembered primarily and unfairly as the man who copped both barrels from the 1982 Kangaroo tourists – the first to win every match in Britain and still the biggest shock to the system that the game in this country has ever had. As Great Britain coach, he had to make all the subsequently embarrassing confident predictions that there was nothing to fear, but he probably knew differently when he found that, despite pushing 52 at the time, he performed rather better in training than some of his forwards.

Johnny still runs a gym and trains a wide range of sportsmen, notably marathon runners and kickboxers, neither of whom have exactly taken the easy option. But with them, as with his rugby players, he has what seems, to modern sensibilities, one very strange foible. You can't go to a rugby league match, certainly since the switch to a summer season, without noticing that the contemporary player routinely takes on board gallons of water over the 80 minutes. In fact, some water-carriers spend longer on the pitch than the players. To Whiteley, it's all a symptom of modern decadence and decline. He never drinks a drop during training and doesn't think anyone else should either. If they do, it's a sign of weakness; the first man to ask for water will be the first one to run out of the trench and away from the battle. In his 70s, he's not a bad advert for this unfashionably arid approach, but it makes me wonder whether the 1982 Test team wasn't just out-played and out-fought by Australia but also suffering from dehydration. They were certainly out-drunk, because I can't remember the Kangaroos turning down a glass of anything on that tour.

Johnny's hard-line philosophy on this matter made him the only person on a hot day in Hull who was not grateful for the ministrations of Graham. Now, thanks to Tesco, we were not exactly short of cold cans and bottles of all descriptions; we probably had enough for the dozens of people walking with us. But I have a rule when walking in temperatures above 25 degrees: never refuse a drink unless you know for a fact that it's poisonous. That was where Graham came in. As a Hull fan on his own turf, he saw it as his duty of hospitality to be lurking around every corner, car boot up and refreshing, ice-cold beverages ready for the drinking. I had Gentleman Johnny Whiteley's share.

* * *

Fittingly, our route out of Hull takes us between the old and the new, the past and the future, The Boulevard and the shiny KC Stadium. There can have been few more emotional nights in rugby league than the night they closed the old place down, with the Kiwis doing an extra haka at full-time to the strains of 'Old Faithful', the best song in rugby league. Unlike the end of Central Park, for instance, it was an upbeat occasion, with a sense that it was time to move on. It helps, of course, when you're only moving around the corner, to a stadium with a far better view of the action and no need to change your match-day routine.

The Boulevard was a place with an atmosphere all its own, though, and not always a pleasant one. The abuse from the Threepenny Stand was the most intense and the most personal – ask a few ex-Hull players – in the game. There was a nasty tendency towards racial animosity, despite the part that black men like Roy Francis and Clive Sullivan – one of the few in rugby league to have a road, not a poxy little street, mind, but a main route in and out of the city, named after him – played in their history. 'He's not black, he's black-and-white,' one ritually abused black player was told about Sullivan. Following a pitch invasion at Huddersfield after the Challenge Cup semi-final defeat by Leeds in 2000, the club made a concerted attempt to sort out its problem with a minority of its supporters, with innovations like ambassadors appointed to welcome visiting fans. The KC Stadium will be a good test for the nature-versus-nurture argument which says that, if you put people in a decent environment, they will behave decently. Letters to the rugby league press suggest that you can still get a fair old gobful in some parts of the new stadium and the reception we get in the supporters' bar is as raucous as anything at The Boulevard; Stevo wisely settled for leading a chorus of 'Old Faithful', the sentimental little cowboy song that they love so much, but the new place could never be as intimidating as its predecessor. Not that they have jettisoned their history, though. In the leafy surrounds of the new stadium, you can buy a raffle ticket for a proudly displayed garden shed, although that description hardly does it justice. It is designed as a garden shed in the same sense that the *Mona Lisa* would pass muster as a passport photo, adorned as it is with full-length portraits of Hull's notional best-ever team: Whiteley, Harris and the Drakes from their era; Sullivan, of course; Sterling, Leuluai, Garry Schofield and Lee Crooks from more recent times. Inside, it is their dressing-room, with their named shirts waiting on their hooks. It feels more like a shrine than a shed. It is not a concept that would work everywhere, but at Hull they are queuing up, as they were when they unveiled a memorial to Jack Harrison, whose heroic demise in the First World War made him rugby league's only recipient of the Victoria Cross.

The Boulevard still stands and still gets some use for amateur games and greyhounds, but the departure of Hull FC has unmistakably hastened the decline of a neighbourhood that Shaun McRae describes as 'Beirut without the bombs'. The famous Airlie Street chippy was already closed down, driven out, its last proprietor told me, by 'bricks through the windows from the smack-heads'. (Mind you, I always had my doubts about their business acumen. Fish and chips were £1.20; fish, chips and peas only £1.)

It's hard to think that, long after it was built and like other grounds in St Helens, Halifax, Salford, Leeds and Bradford, for instance, it was still in the heart of the respectable suburbs. Now that the club has moved, even just half a mile away, with a Kurdistani takeaway – the first one I'd ever seen – nearby, there is nothing to hold the immediate area together. I suppose that, if you live in Fulham or Chelsea, a football or rugby ground might seem to lower the tone; in parts of Rugby League Land it is the only thing that keeps it up.

* * *

McRae nods towards what appears to be a drugs deal being transacted in a doorway, but you don't go far down Anlaby Road before you are in suburbia, where people in carpet slippers and Hull replica shirts come down their garden paths to throw coins in the buckets. This was the area to which I was brought by my friend, Niel Wood, after that Embassy versus Kazan match the previous December to see what he promised me were the most over-the-top displays of Christmas lights in the Northern Union. He wasn't wrong; some of the best featured not only banks of lights up the fronts, backs and sides of the houses, but also life-sized reindeer traipsing across the roofs and rotund Santas shinning up and down the chimney pots.

I've never seen anything in England to match it, although Barbados' exuberant approach to the festive season came close.

Straight on at the fork in the road would take us through the Ellas – East Ella, West Ella, Kirk Ella – that denote different gradations of suburban comfort. 'I'll be a different sort of fella,' sings Mike Waterson's aspiring trawlerman. 'I'll have a house out in Kirk Ella. And I'll show the bleedin' neighbours who's a man.' The left fork, however, takes us past Boothferry Park, now empty following Hull City's move to share the KC, but in 1982 the scene of the first Test, when Australia – featuring another Ella, Steve, on the bench – put 40 points past Great Britain and we discovered that we did have something to fear after all. John Whiteley winces, just ever so slightly, as we pass. The Kangaroos were pushed much harder on that tour by Hull, with Mick Crane – a player who embodied that Three Day Millionaire philosophy – playing his way into the Great Britain team for the third Test with the sort of old-fashioned English ball-handling that made us think we had nothing to fear. Hull were so strong in those days that they could sometimes afford to leave Crane out of the side, particularly if he had gone missing recently, as they did for one Wembley final. They were making a video of the trip and the breathless interviewer asked him: 'Here we are, going down Wembley Way for the biggest game of your career. Aren't you nervous?'

'I aren't nervous,' he said, probably drawing on his fag. 'I aren't playing.'

* * *

We go through Hessle, a village I remember, from staying there once during the World Cup, for having the longest lists of people banned from pubs that I have ever seen posted up. They went from ceiling to floor, with three or four generations of some families represented. If there is a disappointment on this leg of the journey, apart from the fact that my turn pushing Scott's wheelchair precludes me from checking whether there have been any late additions, it is that there is not much of a view of the Humber Bridge – the most spectacular structure on the whole of the route. When it was opened in 1981 – it was a busy couple of years in Hull – it was the longest single-span bridge in the world at 1,419 metres, since overtaken by one in Japan. That is disappointing in this city of superlatives and makes you wonder what might come next. Not a bigger haddock from Grimsby, I trust. Superseded it might be, but it still dwarfs puny efforts like the Golden Gate in San Francisco as it guards the way into the city from the west by road and rail, as well as linking the north and south banks of the Humber. It never made them think or feel like one county, though; Lincolnshire, despite its proximity to Hull, has remained stubbornly immune to the attractions of rugby league. Walking across its footway can be bracing, to say the least, and the bridge is sometimes closed to traffic because of high winds that could easily carry off a small family saloon.

Graham, of whose Lemon Barley Water I have by this stage drunk quantities that would do justice to a Wimbledon finalist, once saw someone taken off the bridge by other forces. He was working underneath with a council gang one day when he happened to look up and saw a motorcyclist pull up, remove his helmet and leathers, stack them neatly and dive into the Humber. He phoned the police and told them what he had seen. 'No, you didn't,' they told him when they arrived on the scene. 'You saw him skid, lose control and go flying over the parapet.' No, Graham said, he'd seen the fellow strip off and dive in. No, he was told more firmly this time. If he insisted that he saw that, his widow wouldn't get a bean. So he didn't see it, although how the unfortunate biker left all his gear behind as he plunged to his death must have taken some explaining.

Beyond Hessle, the houses are often huge, with room for a row or two of the back-to-backs that surround The Boulevard in their front gardens, and a reminder that there was plenty of money made in Kingston upon Hull when the wool went out and the fish came in. This is also the natural home for Hull rugby league aristocracy; both McRae and Whiteley live in Swanland, which was traditionally (and appropriately in Johnny's case) a dry village, but which now has a welcome watering-hole overlooking a picture postcard duckpond. There is a slight curl of the gentlemanly lip as walkers made of less stern stuff take liquids on board like the potential deserters they are.

A little further on, in Welton, there is an inn, the Green Dragon, with Dick Turpin connections, as one of his many supposed hiding places and, according to some versions, the one where he was finally caught. They remember another folk hero around these parts as well.

'Greg Mackey used to live behind there,' says someone walking along with us, recalling the Australian stand-off who was Hull's captain and man of the match when they won the Premiership Trophy in 1991 – their last major prize. 'I gave him a lift home one night. He spewed up in the back of my van.'

* * *

Talking of highwaymen and lovable rogues, this was the stretch of road where we almost lost Stevo, before he had even got into his stride. Calling into a village shop to buy a birthday card, he fell way behind the peloton. How long does it take to buy a birthday card, I hear you ask? Well, anything up to half an hour, if it involves long, rambling conversations with the sub-postmistress and anyone else who happens to be around, and generally putting on the command performance that goes with the territory – and that's before you even stick the stamp on and post it. The result was that he was almost a mile behind and that Irish Phil, who had already discovered that walking wasn't for him at all, at all, drove back in one of the support vehicles to offer him a lift.

'Sure, there's no one would know,' he said. But Stevo was having none of it. He pulled up his socks, rolled up his sleeves, set his jaw and set about making up lost ground. Like the smell of rotten fish, he was not to be easily shaken off.

II

Viva Cas Vegas!

A ONE-TIME TEAMMATE I TOLD ABOUT OUR PROPOSED ROUTE has been indirectly responsible for belatedly persuading me that the time for playing the game has finally passed me by. It was when I saw him taping protective padding over his pierced nipple before a match that I knew beyond doubt I was out of my era. But I am guilty of deviation – as, I'm beginning to think, is he. 'Ponte Carlo and Cas Vegas,' he said, 'Tha'll a' thissen a good doh.' Not only is he a native of those parts, but, as you will have guessed, a part-time elocution teacher.

Pontefract was not on our itinerary, which was a shame, because it provided the inspiration for another of John Godber's best-known plays, *Bouncers*. It was based on Kiko's, which used to boast proudly of being 'Yorkshire's only Polynesian Nightspot' – as opposed to the many in Lancashire – and numbered Viv 'Spend, Spend, Spend' Nicholson among its regulars. Its doormen were largely recruited from the willing ranks of rugby league players, which is just as well, because Pontefract's boisterous nightlife is as famous as its cakes, made until recently from locally grown liquorice. I once arrived in the early evening in a marketplace that had more than a touch of Ye Olde Englishe about it; until, that was, you spotted a Black Maria parked around each of its corners, waiting for the inevitable custom from the compulsory battles between what were then mining villages like Featherstone and Sharlston. There was virtually a timetable for who battled whom, when and in which pub, and, if you knew the form, you could avoid it.

Deprived of that experience, we had to make the best of the more refined pleasures of Castleford. There is one thing wrong with it as a town, however, and it is not really its fault; it's a bloody long way from Hull, or it is when you're walking it. There are few landmarks, it's flat – which makes it easier but more boring – and there were few people walking along with us, because we were in the middle of nowhere.

Few people, that is, apart from Ken. I can't remember when I first became aware of his considerable presence, but he was part of the landscape for most of the journey. A Leeds fan, he told me he designed supermarkets for Morrisons, despite his dyslexia. Because he was never taught properly to read at school, he got around that small handicap by learning the Bible from beginning to end, so that when called upon to 'read' he could do so from memory. He could read plans, blueprints and books about supermarket design, he told me, because he recognised the shapes of the relevant words, but not a novel, because he wouldn't know what to expect from that. I wonder how he will fare with this book, whether it will seem to him more akin to story-telling or shelf-stacking.

Ken announced that he was going to do the whole trek with us, but it wasn't as simple as that. He might well have done the 220 miles, but he did it in a different order, sometimes backwards and often in the middle of the night. Although he was usually the slowest in the party, he reckoned to walk 50 miles at a stretch on his nocturnal forays. He would turn up, in the middle of the moors or down some obscure side street, having just walked the bit we were about to do, or about to attack the section we had just finished. Sometimes he would walk the same route as us for a few hours and then have to dash off to design a supermarket, returning later to tick off the remaining miles. I wasn't certain whether his dyslexia extended to map-reading or not, but I had no trouble believing the rest of his cover story. There's a Morrisons near us and it looks exactly as though it was designed by a dyslexic insomniac, even though I understand it's not one of his.

If Ken is reading, I can tell him that he came with us through Brough, Elloughton and Ellerker, across Walling Fen to Newport, Scalby and Gilberdyke, names full of East Yorkshire resonance. By Newport, we were being bypassed by the M62, which gives up the ghost and becomes a dual carriageway ten miles before Hull. We cross the motorway for the first time at Balkholme Common, with the spires of the cathedral-sized church in Howden looming large on the flat horizon. Like Beverley, to the north of Hull, Howden must once have been vastly more important than it is now, where its Minster dwarfs everything. It does have, however, a new industry of sorts to replace the wool upon which East Yorkshire's old prosperity was based. It has been, for the last few years, the home of the Press Association, making it the true hub of the nation's news-gathering and dissemination, far more so than a mythologised thoroughfare like Fleet Street or even its successor, Canary Wharf. When I need to phone through a match report to *The Independent*, for instance, I speak not to the Docklands, but to Howden, probably to a Hull lass, who might be slightly wrong-footed by the funny way I pronounce 'phone' or 'Charlie Stone', but who will always know how to spell James Leuluai and how many 'r's there are in Garreth Carvell. Howden also has a pub named after Barnes Wallis, the inventor of the bouncing bomb, but, being a couple of miles out of town next to the station, it is so far off our route that it might as well be near one of the dams on the Ruhr he was responsible for flattening. Sky's camera crews stop us regularly at pubs to film footage making great play on how tough it is for me and Stevo to go past their welcoming portals, but they are always pubs which are shut.

The first time you really feel as though you are getting anywhere on this route is when you cross the River Ouse, which has just stopped being the Humber and has started oozing its way up towards York. The vast majority of traffic now uses the modern motorway bridge, but Stevo, for one, can remember when the Boothferry Bridge, which now looks like something thrown up temporarily by the Royal Engineers, was the only crossing if you were on your way to Hull for an away game. From there, our route ahead looks suspiciously like a series of power stations. These ponderous additions to the British landscape seem to compete with each other for the most idyllically pastoral names, sounding for all the world like the sort of place you would go on holiday: Ferrybridge; Fiddler's Ferry near Widnes; the various names under which Windscale/Sellafield has blotted the Cumbrian coast – it will surely be known as Sunny Sands before it's finished reprocessing. The refreshing exception is the one immediately in front of us. Drax sounds like something out of science fiction, or an acronym for something too horrible to spell out. In fact, it's just the name of the village in the shadow of its cooling towers and chimneys – one of which, at 259 metres, is the tallest in the country; two villages, to be precise, Drax and Long Drax.

Dave was a fitter at Drax B, although we thought, when he started chasing us along the country lanes thereabouts, that he might be some deranged farmer whose livestock we had inadvertently startled. In fact, he was the life president of the Drax branch of the Stevo Fan Club and we were delayed for some time whilst he took full advantage of the opportunity to tackle his hero on the burning issues of the day, like 'Yer mate, Eddie Hemmings . . . does he black it, his hair?' Let nobody say that Sky has failed to raise the intellectual level of debate within the game. Dave finds himself temporarily embarrassed for cash, but promises to catch us up later. When we had just about given up on him, he screeches to a halt in the middle of Rawcliffe – village green, maypole – with a tenner filched from his wife's purse. When he tells her the low-down on the hair-dyeing question, she will no doubt consider it money well spent. Just through the small town of Snaith, there are the villages of Great Heck and Little Heck, amusing enough towards the end of a long day in the sun, but slightly less hilarious in 2001 when a driver nodded off at the wheel on the M62 and went over the embankment onto the railway line, causing a derailment which killed ten. Road safety was very much in our minds at this stage, with several miles of walking towards oncoming lorries on the way to Eggborough – another place-name straight out of children's television, but notable mainly for its power station. Uncle Bernard had emerged as a hard taskmaster, but he had held out the promise of a pint in the pub there. As we drew closer, dodging the HGVs, it was obvious that something was wrong. We soon found out what the whispers meant; the Horse and Jockey was closed, which could have been the cue for mutiny. Uncle Bernard's native ingenuity came to the rescue, simply driving to the nearest off-licence and bringing back cans to drink in the beer garden until the landlady took the unsubtle hint and opened up.

By this stage, we are back on the rugby league map, something underlined by the mums and kids in their Castleford shirts who are there to walk with us the following morning. Also by this stage, I had developed something of an obsession with getting off-road, with getting a break from the endless tarmac. It had worked well the previous day, with a short but refreshing detour along a riverside embankment in the village of Airmyn; it was less impressive in Eggborough, as I led the whole party through a gap in a hedge and up a cul-de-sac.

After that, I let the locals lead the way to Knottingley, a place I'd always imagined as some sort of earthly paradise, given the reluctance of Paul Newlove to leave it for ball-aching experiences like Great Britain tours to Australia. Well, it isn't quite that, but it does have a few things going for it, like a restored Roman amphitheatre you can hire for parties and functions and a high-class café, which kindly provided the whole party with bacon barm-cakes. At least, that might have been what they called them. Across the north of England, the name by which a roundish, flattish lump of bread is called operates as a series of shibboleths. In Bolton, it's a barmcake, but, if I go ten miles away and ask for such a thing, they will look at me as if I have dropped from Mars and have demanded a live baby to eat. There, it will be a breadcake, a flourcake, a teacake, a bap or a bun; if you play for the Gateshead Thunder, you will have to learn to call it a stottie, which is right off the graph. I am indebted to John Kear – an expert on the subject – for the information that, in Castleford, a shuffler is a triangular barmcake, particularly suitable for holding fillets of fish from the chippy. And as for oven bottoms . . . better, I think, not even to go there. If you ask for it by the wrong name, you might as well be speaking in Swahili. I know about these matters; my dad used to bake them by the millions and never knew what the hell to call them. In Perth and

Sydney, thousands of miles apart, they have the same names for all the same things. Here, you keep walking for a little further than usual and you encounter mute incomprehension. Anyway, they were very nice and, in the window of the café, there was a poster advertising the start of pre-season training for Knottingley Rockware Under 8s, at the cutely named Sleepy Valley – probably in the shadow of a power station.

On the way to the next collection of cooling towers at Ferrybridge, I noticed that I was falling behind the pace. For this, I blame not any excessive consumption of barms, baps or buns, but Sally from the souvenir shop. Apart from the fact that she had been forced to shed her ill-fitting trainers and was walking painfully in her socks, hers was the sort of story that couldn't be rushed. Although she once played in a hockey team with the redoubtable Kath Hetherington, the chairperson (it says in their programme) of Hull, Sally is what I would call rock-solid rugby league – and Castleford in particular. She struggles along bringing up her three children on her own, since her husband cleared off, and takes her only couple of hours off from that task to watch her team every week – even then helping out in the club shop. One of her twin daughters needs her appendix removing and her son, walking with us, has a bowel condition and shouldn't really play rugby league. 'They said it could kill him if he gets hit the wrong way, but he just loves it so much. You can get killed crossing the road, can't you?' Sally has already collected no end of money for the Trek and proves our most enthusiastic bucket-wielder so far. When I find out, some days later, that the bacon barms were actually bought and paid for by her, I almost curl up and die of embarrassment on the spot. I'll be buying something from the souvenir shop at The Jungle, whether I want it or not.

There are few towns as synonymous with their rugby league club as Castleford, or few places as little known for anything else. This is a little unfair. Cas, as Lagentium, was an important Roman settlement, where they built a fort to guard a ford over the River Aire, and, rather more recently, the birthplace in 1898 and early home of one of Britain's greatest sculptors, Henry Moore. As far as I know, none of his many works draws on the town's sporting heritage, but his *Draped Reclining Figure* stands, or rather reclines, outside the Civic Centre. It has fared rather better than a family group of his in Harlow new town, Essex, where vandals, or art critics, have removed the baby's head on several occasions.

* * *

They produce a few other things in Castleford, like 'flour with nowt taken out' and clothes with the Burberry trademark, which used to have a slightly posh aura of huntin', fishin' and shootin', but now seem to be the garments of choice for the well-dressed football hooligan. The main exports, however, always used to be coal and rugby league players. Cas was surrounded by pits and the Miners' Strike was as bitter here as anywhere, with memories of who was on which side festering to this day. They have all gone now and someone like the recently retired Cas stalwart, Dean Sampson, who grew up in nearby Stanley, says that the loss of one staple is a threat to the other. Castleford and its hinterland have all the typical problems – long-term unemployment, crime, drugs – of ex-coalfield areas. 'The lifestyle in a lot of areas around here isn't conducive to being a full-time sportsman,' he says. 'The disciplines of earning a living have gone out of the window.' It hasn't stopped the flow of rugby players yet, but there is not the high proportion of Castleford-bred players fleshing out clubs in West Yorkshire and beyond that there used to be. It doesn't mean that there is a lack of ingenuity in the town, either, as Andy and Bernard found out when they were researching our route. Spotting some local loafer, some indigenous idler, they asked him if he could give them directions. He'd do better than that, he said, he'd hop in and guide them. It was only when they'd dropped him off that they realised they were nowhere near where they wanted to be, but had conveniently deposited him at his chosen pub, ready to start his day's drinking 20 minutes early.

I once spent the best part of two weeks in Castleford, working with Neville Smith, later the mastermind behind Sky's coverage of the game, on a television film about Australian players in Britain, by the end of which I felt that I had exhausted most of its possibilities. I never did visit the nightclub, though, in which Dean Sampson once woke up in a cubicle in the gents at four in the morning after a 'team bonding' session and had to phone the police to let him out. I notice that the town centre has now acquired a Thai restaurant, which is something of a barometer of sophistication. Back in the 1980s, however, my mission involved spending a good deal of time in The Ship, a big Tetley's pub on the main roundabout in the middle of town that was the traditional gathering place for players. In the days before full-time professionalism, it was the magnet on Tuesday and Thursday nights for Castleford-based players who were with the Hull clubs, Leeds, Bradford or whoever, as well as those with their home-town team, to gather there after training. You could not have had a better illustration of the disproportionate wealth of playing ability in one small town; on a good night, you could have picked half a dozen decent teams.

The Ship is boarded up now and seems to have been absorbed into the motorcycle showrooms next door, but there is an instructive side-trip to be made, over the old bridge, built in 1808, that crosses the Calder – or is it the Aire? They do a complicated, intertwining dance with each other around these parts, with the Aire and Calder Navigation thrown into the mix just to confuse things further, although it was the Calder that was supposed to lend its name to the merged Castleford/Featherstone/Wakefield club that was part of the original Super League blueprint – the one that was never going to happen. Maybe it was the name that was the problem; they might have done better building castles on the Aire.

Down the backstreets is a ground that ranks alongside Sleepy Valley as West Yorkshire's leader in the evocative-name stakes – The Sandy Desert. This field – deserted but not especially sandy – is now used by Lock Lane second XIII, but it was Castleford's original ground when they became a professional club in 1926, before they moved to Wheldon Road, home of the town's ailing soccer club, a year later.

A pleasant stroll further upstream takes you to The Boat in the village of Allerton Bywater – which produced, among many others, Malcolm Reilly. There are several good reasons for abandoning The Ship for The Boat. For starters, it is an excellent pub, which brews its own delectable beer in outbuildings at the back. By way of a link with the start of the walk, as if I needed one, The Minerva in Hull regularly sells one of its brews, with a picture on the pump-clip of The Boat's landlord, Brian Lockwood.

Lockwood was one of the great forwards of his era, which stretched from the late '60s to the early '80s, achieving great success with a string of clubs, including winning the Challenge Cup with Castleford, Hull KR and Widnes, winning Tests and a World Cup with Great Britain and playing in Australia for Balmain and Canterbury. He is also an outstanding example of a classic rugby league type – the Disgruntled Ex-Player, whose love–hate relationship with the game seems to have run a little short on the love. On a trip where just about everyone you come across is self-selected for a pretty upbeat view of rugby league, it seemed only fair and balanced to meet Locky as well.

Although he was born into a rugby league family, that love–hate relationship was there from the start. 'Castleford offered me £200 to sign and my mum offered me £200 out of her own pocket not to. She'd just seen so many cuts and bangs.' He did sign, but Cas were supposed to keep it quiet so that he could play for Yorkshire as an amateur. They let the cat out of the bag and he missed that opportunity, but he had already had a meeting that underlined the close-knit nature of the game, playing against Roger Millward – a classic case of a Castleford lad who had to leave to fulfil his potential – before he found out that he was his cousin.

During his playing career, Lockwood was never a social animal, never a regular at The Ship. Even now, sitting out on the riverbank outside his pub, he doesn't drink his own beer; he had a single bottle of Beck's a couple of weeks earlier and suffered from dehydration for days.

As a professional, Lockwood was the sharpest of operators in an era when, before the introduction of guaranteed contract payments, it was a case of survival of the fittest off the field as well as on it. Players – the ones good enough to get away with it – were in a process of constant negotiation with their clubs. 'I had money everywhere,' he says. 'In boxes under the bed – everywhere.' And yet his most vivid memories now concern the money he was cheated out of, like the 10 per cent of the fee from Balmain he was promised by Castleford. 'They told me they hadn't got enough for me. I found out later that they'd got £40,000. I never felt the same about Castleford after that.'

Lockwood was a match-winner in Australia as well as in England, with his ball-handling skills and his energy. One of those who fell under his influence was a 16-year-old Ian Millward. 'I went to a touch football session he ran and some of the things he did with the ball I couldn't believe,' says Millward, who has since brought some of the ideas that were triggered by that day into his coaching at Leigh and St Helens. Lockwood also had spells coaching Wakefield and Huddersfield, leaving both clubs because of disputes with the board. 'I found that they treated players like cattle,' he said. Now his expertise, which was as influential in Australia as it was here, is lost to the game. He might watch it on TV from time to time, in between supervising operations at The Boat and playing golf, but that's about it.

Nor does he have any dealings with Castleford, just a mile or so down the road, and thereby hangs a particularly sad but not untypical story. In the late '70s, when he was playing for Hull KR, he and his teammates went to Wheldon Road to see whether Cas could beat Widnes and thus give Rovers the Championship. Everyone was allowed into the players' bar after the game, except Lockwood, who was told that he would have to go and get a ticket. He didn't go for that ticket, a quarter of a century ago. 'And I've never been back since,' he says.

* * *

Like a lot of ex-players who fall out with the game, he is cutting off his nose to spite his face. I can't believe that he wouldn't enjoy The Jungle – as Wheldon Road is now known, despite the end of the sponsorship from a dot.com operation that saw its name changed.

There's nothing fancy about the place and the facilities are basic, but the atmosphere is pure rugby league. You approach it down a street of what amounts to rugby league theme bars – the Early Bath is a particular favourite – and, although there might be a couple of dressed-up Tigers revving around the pitch on motorbikes, the tone is set by the kids' game – complete with commentary – and the juvenile dance troop. The team has been known, at least since the '60s, as Classy Cas, and the rugby there is almost always worth watching.

On the night we are there, they pack out the room with fans for a question-and-answer session. Although the season is on its way to a disappointing conclusion, you can feel the enthusiasm in the air. That is despite the disappointment of a piece of news that is typical of Castleford's history: Danny Orr is off to Wigan the following season. It is the fate of many of the town's favourite sons; most of the best move on at some stage, because Cas will always be a small-town club, and they are replaced by the next batch. But losing Orr is particularly hard to take; he's as local as you can be, the son of a Cas player, the club captain and the fulcrum of the side. When he was trying to decide between staying or going to Wigan or Hull, his manager, the ex-Castleford player, former director and now broadcaster, Ron Hill, promised to tip me off – on one condition. 'You sit in front of me in the press box for the first match after it's announced,' he said. So I was Ron Hill's human shield. There was a bit of jeering and pointing, but nothing was thrown and the remaining hostility evaporated when Orr played perhaps the best game of his Castleford career.

In the audience that night at Castleford was John, a chap about my age who had particular reason to be keen on the event. When he was in his teens and, by his own account, a bit of a tearaway, he went on an Outward Bound course. 'The best six weeks of my life,' he said. 'It changed my life completely.' That's the sort of reminder you need from time to time, when your legs are starting to complain about walking 18 miles a day. I don't suppose that the need for what Outward Bound can provide has diminished in Castleford.

* * *

The Duke of Wellington used to have the unadorned address of Number One, London – and the postman never failed to deliver his mail correctly to his house at Hyde Park Corner. If there was an equivalent in these parts, it would be Ray Tennant's house, on the corner plot on our way in, that would be designated as Number One, Castleford. Ray is a former leading referee, who is now in charge of those higher-tech sources of controversy, the video referees. He also owns the shop that pioneered the merchandising of rugby league, selling all manner of stuff related to the game long before most clubs had the same idea. He invites us into his patioed back garden, complete with waterfall, for pizza and pasta, and the scene, with the extended family, babies, dogs, cats and passers-by, is more reminiscent of the Mediterranean than the Aire and Calder Navigation. At least, that was the way it seemed at the time; but we did make a video of the event and, having watched it several times from different angles, in freeze-frame and super slo-mo, I'm no longer quite so sure.

* * *

At Ray's shop, we all change into different T-shirts. It is one aspect of the Trek to which I had given little thought – this need to be correctly attired at all times. Every night, we are given instructions about the following day's kit – one of the senses, I suppose, in which the experience reminds Phil and Stevo of Great Britain tours. Things weren't quite as organised for those of us on tour merely to write about it. On the Trek, it's all about giving the requisite local publicity to the various supporters of the venture. I still have the Tesco trolley-pusher's T-shirt into which I squeezed for promotional pictures at one supermarket, but I have promised the children that I will not wear it again on a night out. I would have thought it had a certain cachet, but they tell me this is not the case.

At Ray's we change into the shirts he has provided and out of them again when we arrive at Castleford's club shop in the Carlton Lanes shopping centre. The place is clogged with fans and with Castleford players doing their bit to speed us on our way. Danny Orr is there with his baby son; so are players like Andy Lynch, Wayne Godwin and Tom Saxton upon whom the future of the club will depend. What Brian Lockwood calls 'the production line' might not run at quite the pace it once did, but it is a hell of a long way from grinding to a halt.

Everywhere in Britain has something like Carlton Lanes. It takes the club shop to show you that you are in Castleford – an illustration of the theory that clubs are becoming more rather than less important in preserving the identity of their towns and cities in an era of increasing homogeneity. You are certainly in no doubt just where you are in the world when the girls in the shop get hold of you for a face-paint job. Phil is transformed into a rather unconvincingly fierce Tiger, more like something from an off-Broadway production of *Cats*, and Stevo into an interesting cross between a Maori warrior and the man in the Tango advert. A beard presents a different set of technical problems for the ladies with the pigments; they don't come across many of them when they regularly transform several dozen school-age Castleford fans before every home game. I also pointed out that, as we are due to set off from what the Romans used to call Classy Lagentium for Wakefield in five minutes and 38 seconds – Uncle Bernard's timing – I would really prefer something a little more non-sectarian. 'Give him the half-and-half,' says the boss, which sounds fine until I look in the mirror and find that it consists of the familiar home strip of amber, black and white down one side, beard and all, and the most popular recent change kit of green and black down the other. Tasteful, but not exactly even-handed.

I got most of the paint off in the gents' toilets at the Rising Sun in Whitwood, because I wasn't walking into Wakefield identified, not once but twice, as a Castleford supporter. I'd like to apologise now to the landlord of that establishment for leaving him with a towel which is probably still amber down one side and green down the other.

Another question of identity arose later that day. As we were driving two young girls back to Knottingley, where they had joined us on the walk that morning, we got to talking about how impressive the turn-out of Cas players had been that lunchtime – all of them resplendent in their club gear.

'All except Danny Orr,' said one of them, picking out the one player who happened to be in civvies, which had given him a slightly semi-detached look. 'Ah well,' said the other with the wisdom of the ages, echoing sentiments that must have been expressed in similar terms every time a home-town hero has left. 'He isn't a real Castleford player any more.'

III

Wakefield: Every Play a Mystery

IT'S ONLY A SHORT STROLL FROM CASTLEFORD TO WAKEFIELD
on our preordained route. If I'd have been planning it, I wouldn't
have gone that way – and if we had a quid for every time between
Hull and Widnes that someone told us that, Outward Bound would
be able to send the whole population of these islands to the Lake
District – but would have detoured through Featherstone and
Sharlston. Fev, to give it its chummy abbreviation, is a more extreme
example of the ability, seen in Castleford, of a small community to
keep a disproportionately important club going. Featherstone is
only an overgrown village and Super League might be a distant
prospect for it now, but it kept a club in the top flight, winning cups
and championships, for longer than should be possible. Someone
once proved that the proportion of its modest population that went
to matches put to shame dilettante operations like the football club
in Burnley. It would probably be the best place on our entire route
– or just off it – to start a riot by standing in the main street and
shouting out what a good thing Super League has been. The belief
here that they have been done down by marketing men and
administrators in shiny suits, for whom rugby in pit villages was not
the object of the exercise, is stronger than anywhere in Rugby
League Land. It is an article of faith which is a long way from being
without foundation and it taps into a deep seam of local militancy.

On the main street, briefly visible as we drive past, is a sculpture marking the centenary of the Featherstone Massacre, when two striking miners were shot by soldiers in 1893. At the crossroads, there is a bas-relief depicting the two things that have any significance in Featherstone's history – coal mining and rugby league. With the pits long gone, parts of the village now hark back again to its older, more rural roots, although other parts of it now feel disappointingly like a dormitory suburb for Leeds. From the stand at Post Office Road – one of rugby league's more evocative addresses, although the post office is now relocated down the main street – the only scenes of human activity you can see are farmers' fields. It can be an oddly peaceful place, as it was a few weeks after the walk, when I went there to help scatter my friend Peter Ward's ashes on the pitch. He had watched Rovers from his boyhood so it was where his widow, Jean, thought he should be and the only sound was the dull thud of rugby balls being kicked on the practice pitch nearby.

Anyway, we were not walking this way, nor through Sharlston, a little further down the road. The tidy Sharlston Rovers ground is a reminder of the remarkable rugby heritage of this even smaller village. Among the many players it has produced are the Fox brothers: Neil, the Wakefield Trinity and Great Britain centre and, like another Sharlston man, Jonty Parkin, a member of the Rugby League Hall of Fame; Peter, an average player, by his own admission, but the most successful coach of his generation; and Don, a fine player cruelly and invidiously remembered only for the easy, but missed, conversion that cost Trinity the 1968 Challenge Cup final. To add insult to injury, he was interviewed live on the Wembley pitch moments afterwards by David Coleman, who tried to cheer him up by telling him that he had won the Lance Todd Trophy as man of the match – the third from Sharlston, after brother Neil and Featherstone's Carl Dooler, to achieve that in a single decade, although Coleman didn't go into that. Don's stricken expression on hearing the good news has never quite left him. On this occasion, Eddie Waring got it right. 'Poor lad,' he said and left it at that.

* * *

Our route on foot takes us instead past the designer outlet village – whatever that is – of Freeport and across the M62 to Normanton, in the company of that town's most notable rugby league son, David Topliss. He ranks among Hull's finest – his picture is on that garden shed as their best-ever stand-off – but the bulk of his career was spent playing for or coaching Wakefield. He served seven years in that latter role, with the signing of Henry Paul from the Junior Kiwi tour one of his major coups, before deciding in 1994 to take a short break; he is still taking it. 'The problem was that the game was becoming full-time and, at the time, I had a good business. I thought I'd take a step back, but once I did that there was no way back in,' he says. Although he has dabbled around the edges since then, his active involvement is now limited to playing a mean game of touch rugby – at which discipline I can vouch for his continued elusiveness – and watching his son-in-law, Wayne McDonald, play for Leeds.

As luck would have it, he is able, just a little further along the route, to point out the new flat that Wayne has just bought at Heath Common, one of the most surprising spots in Yorkshire. Drop an alien there and tell him that he is only a couple of miles from the middle of an industrial city and he would not believe you. The great sweep of common land is a survival from a completely different way of life, as are the sandstone-built village and gas-lit pub, the King's Arms, that overlook it. It was in the King's Arms, on my last visit, that Dean Sampson's mobile phone had rung, halfway through his third pint, to ask him to make a comeback for Castleford at the age of 36. He squinted at the text message in the gaslight – a clash of technologies if ever there was one – and said 'Never got that one.' He succumbed soon enough, though.

Wakefield Trinity – named after Holy Trinity Church – played their first games in 1873 on Heath Common, although nobody is quite sure where. There is an awful lot of it to choose from, with only a few tethered gypsy horses to share it. The shock to the system, walking in from this direction, is that Belle Vue, their home since 1879, is so close; past the remains of the power station and under the railway bridge and there it is.

If you want to see Belle Vue in its glory, it is no good going now, although the ambience is slightly better than it would have been if the threat had been carried out a couple of years ago, to repossess the stack of Portakabins behind the sticks that constitute its hospitality facilities. No, the answer is to go to the video shop and rent a copy of *This Sporting Life*, which was filmed there in 1962, when Trinity were as glamorous as rugby league got and Belle Vue was a ground to match.

Keith Holliday was the scrum-half in those days and he remembers the film crews descending on Wakefield. 'We'd never seen anything like it. The thing I remember most is the swearing. That Richard Harris, he was a bugger for it. I mean, everyone swears sometimes and nowadays you hear it all the time, but we'd never heard anything like it. I think he was putting himself into the role.'

That role was as Arthur Machin, an injured rugby league player looking back on his career. 'That's the point of the film that a lot of people miss. He's looking back at what happened to him.'

Things happened to Harris at Wakefield when he started to immerse himself in the part. 'Derek Turner came around the scrum and stiff-armed him. No one really liked Richard Harris at the time, so Derek came round and gave him a beauty. But that was Derek – he did that even when he was playing touch and pass; that was the way he was.'

Despite the unpromising start and a mouth that made miners blush, Harris gradually won over the players who were most involved in the making of the film. Most of the filming was done at Belle Vue, with extras getting the then handsome fee of £2 10s to stand on the terraces and cheer. The club secretary used to let Holliday's wife in to get paid and let her out the other gate so that she could go to their nearby home and carry on with her house-work. The Hollidays were even paid a retainer for letting the crew store their cameras in the hallway.

Some of the filming was done further afield, as when the whole crew decamped to Rugby School – William Webb Ellis and all that – for the scene in the communal bath. That took four days and, by the end of it, Wakefield must have been the cleanest team in the league.

When Trinity went to Wembley to play Huddersfield in 1962,

Harris went with them and set his heart on Holliday's bloodstained shirt. '"Give us your shirt," he said, so I said, "Give us your jacket then." He had one of those real big sheepskin jackets. You just didn't see them in those days.'

The swap was done, but the following year, when Wakefield – the Cup specialists of their day – played Wigan, Harris was there again and presented Holliday with a parcel containing the previous year's Wembley shirt. 'He knew I'd got three children and that was a shirt for each of them. The only trouble was that I hadn't still got his jacket. I'd given it to our secretary, because I thought it would be handy for nipping in and out of the office in cold weather. But he said it was all right; he hadn't given me the shirt back to get his jacket back.'

Holliday still has a video of *This Sporting Life*, which he watches occasionally. To him, the rugby action in the film looks staged, as it probably would if you had been there at the time and knew how long it had taken to film. To me, it looks very much as I remember the game in those days; slower, grainier and in black and white. *The Sunday Times Guide to Movies on Television* is on my side. It calls the rugby sequences 'the best sporting photography ever seen', although this is the 1973 edition, before *Escape to Victory* and *When Saturday Comes*.

Where the film scores – and so many sporting films fail – is in getting the atmosphere right. That and the personalities: there's the weaselly reporter, played by Leonard Rossiter; the pompous chairman (with Arthur Lowe trying out some of the mannerisms that were later to define Capt. Mainwaring in *Dad's Army*); and the actor who Keith calls 'that fellow who kept going into the phone box and changing' – the very first Doctor Who (if you accept that there was more than one), William Hartnell. The screenplay – by David Storey, who paid his way through art school by playing full-back in Leeds A team, and based on his 1960 novel – has about it the ring of truth paid for by personal experience.

There is something about Wakefield that inspires drama and fiction, right from the cycle of Mystery Plays – the central mystery of which is death and resurrection, a cycle that Trinity have sometimes seemed destined to go through on an annual basis – and

Oliver Goldsmith's *The Vicar of Wakefield*, through to Alan Plater's *Trinity Tales*, a television reworking of Chaucer's *Canterbury Tales* based on the premise of Wakefield supporters telling each other stories on the way to Wembley. Some things that have actually happened at the club, however, fall into the category of too far-fetched for fiction.

* * *

The drama we were discussing as we approached Belle Vue had unfolded elsewhere. Several weeks earlier, the news had leaked out that a player had failed a drug test and had been fined, given a suspended one-year ban, but not named. The guessing game began. The size of the fine – £2,500 – was a heavy hint that it was a well-paid player from a prominent club. The fact that he had not immediately been suspended and had retained his anonymity suggested, to those of a cynical turn of mind, that he was a player Great Britain needed to have available. Gradually, it became an open secret that the player in question was Keiron Cunningham, the St Helens and Great Britain hooker, who would probably have been, over the previous couple of years, the only British player who would have got into a World XIII. It was such damaging and depressing news that nobody was in a huge rush to write the story, especially as there was no official confirmation that he was the man. On the day we walked towards Wakefield, however, the Rugby League finally spilled the beans.

Cunningham, they revealed, had given a sample which contained traces of HCG, a growth hormone. The relative leniency of the sentence and the initial decision not to name him were because of 'mitigating circumstances', they explained. Those mitigating circumstances emerged later, when Cunningham explained that during his long lay-off with an elbow injury, he had been given the gear by a member of the Great Britain medical staff, who assured him that it was legal. That helpful individual was one Mike Sutherland, who turned out to be a fireman in Bolton, although not one I noticed on the engine the last time we had a blaze down our street, who had convinced the League that he was an expert in the field of nutrition and was acting as a consultant to them. Sutherland had been rumbled in April, but the repercussions had outlived him and his involvement with the RFL explained the kid-glove treatment of Cunningham.

Had you been there as we talked about the implications and walked into Wakefield, you would have noticed an interesting contrast in reactions. Phil Clarke, wearing his hat as Great Britain manager, was just about as fed up as it is possible to be. It's just not something you want to hear about one of your best players with a Test series against Australia looming at the end of the season. I was a lot more cheerful; not because I had anything against Keiron, but because I'd managed to be on holiday for the messiest story of the year – perfect timing.

As luck would have it, Cunningham's first match after being named was due to be at Belle Vue that weekend, so his case was bound to be the hot topic at a fans' forum there that night. Phil played a very straight bat, sticking to his strongly held view that players have to take the responsibility for what they put into their bodies. Also on the panel was the Wakefield coach, Shane McNally, someone I already knew to be highly quotable – and he didn't let us down.

My favourite McNally quote of the season so far had concerned his veteran half-back, Brad Davis, who, with the inevitability of retirement starting to loom on the horizon as he turned 35, had hit the sort of late-flowering form that amounted to an Indian summer. 'By the time you know how to play rugby league,' he said about Davis, 'you're too old to play it any more.' I thought it was one of the wisest things about the game I'd ever heard. Not only did it cut through the usual crap about rugby league being such an easy, simple game, it also summed up the certainty that nags away at us has-beens and never-wases; if only our legs still worked, we would be so much better as players than we were when they did. It's a more comforting thought than anything religion has to say about an afterlife and I will be eternally grateful to him for it. He got it from an old-timer called Bob Richards, with whom he played a third-grade Grand Final in Brisbane, when he was young and impressionable. As we heard that night at Belle Vue, however, pearls of wisdom were not all that the young McNally was offered in dressing-rooms in those days.

Shane tackled the drugs issue as head-on as Phil had. It was out-and-out wrong and should be addressed with longer bans and heavier fines. Mind you, he added, it had always gone on. When he had come on Queensland's 1983 tour to Britain, he said – and I've checked the *Rothmans* and he's there in the middle row of the team picture, complete with hair and beard – he had been shocked to see players who had represented their state and their country popping pills before matches. You look at some of the names involved on that tour and wonder how tarnished some very big reputations from that era should be, not to mention Keiron's in the here and now. He copped for plenty of 'drug cheat' jibes in that match at Wakefield, by the way, but has since acknowledged support from fans of other clubs as well as St Helens.

* * *

We were a mixed bunch the following morning. There were the regulars and the usual sprinkling of injured players. You could form the impression on this journey that everyone in rugby league was injured – which is not far from the truth late in the season – because they were the ones whose training commitments, or lack of them, allowed them to walk with us. This day's walking wounded were Matt Seers and Troy Slattery – two Australians not quite in the class of Wally Lewis, whose arrival in the mid-'80s created such incredulity that the Wakefield fanzine was called *Wally Lewis is Coming*, long after he had been and gone. Also on the move with us were the actor Chris Chittell – the villainous Eric Pollard in *Emmerdale* – and Sir Rodney Walker, once the most powerful man in rugby league and still the possessor of its most powerful handshake. It's a bone-crushing brute of a thing, which can come as a shock to the unwary, but there is a way of dealing with it. You have to thrust your hand deep into his so that you pinion his thumb by the webbing, grab his right wrist with your free hand and compress the tendons in order to deny him maximum leverage. If that fails, you can knee him in the groin, or surrender yourself to the inevitability of him shaking you around like a fox does the severed head of a chicken.

Sir Rodney has been, at various times, the chairman of Wakefield

Trinity, the chairman of the Rugby League, the chairman of the UK Sports Council, the chairman of Manchester's Commonwealth Games Committee – which failed to get any rugby league on the menu at those Games – and the chairman of Leicester City, as well as the chairman of countless other bodies. I have recently read that he has become the chairman of the World Snooker Association. If there was an Association of British Chairmen, he would be the chairman of that. It was as though the whole world was a chair, Sir Rodney was the man who sat in it and rugby league was a little splinter in the seat. I used to wonder how he came to be chairman of so many organisations, but the answer is simple; they decide it by arm-wrestling. I've seen him chair meetings and there is no doubt about his effectiveness. If he isn't getting his own way, he goes around and shakes a few hands and they suddenly start to see things his way. The Rugby League Trek doesn't have a chairman, but, if it did, Sir Rodney would be it; instead, he is the next best thing, its patron – and a generous one to boot. His own boots are not, however, made for much walking. He has to leave after a few hundred yards; he has a meeting to chair.

* * *

By then, we have passed a building I will always associate with one of the more bizarre episodes in Wakefield's history. What could be a more appropriate setting than a church for the leap of faith that was the John Pearman Affair.

Before the 2000 Super League season, the Wildcats – as they were asking us to call them by this stage – announced that their days of financial hardship were behind them. The recruitment of Pearman had opened up a pot of gold and they set about spending it on a whole new team, including expensive signings like Bobbie Goulding and Steve McNamara. The atmosphere that day in the church next door to the ground – Belle Vue then had nowhere adequate for such an occasion – was akin to a revivalist meeting. On top of the players they did recruit, Trinity made the sort of moves that are often descibed in the popular prints as 'audacious' for Jonah Lomu, Andrew and Matthew Johns and Jason Robinson. By April, the cheques for the players who were there in reality, as

51

opposed to in Trinity's dreams, were bouncing all over Yorkshire. By the end of May, they had sacked their coach, Andy Kelly. By the end of July, they had sacked Pearman for failing to come up with the funding he had promised and the contractor was threatening to dismantle the hospitality stand which he had erected but for which he had not been paid. Players over the age of 24 had their contracts ripped up at the end of August. Even by Wakefield's standards, it had been an eventful season. 'He seemed so plausible,' said Trinity's chairman, Ted Richardson, of Pearman. It was an interesting use of the word plausible, to mean 'someone who tells you what you want to hear', which is not a definition I can find in any of my dictionaries. Plausible isn't the word I would use; I shook hands with him.

* * *

Closer to the city centre, there is another, better-known place of worship, the fourteenth-century Chantry Chapel – one of only four of its type in Britain – on the medieval bridge over the Calder. You can walk in, have a look at the stained glass and reflect upon what a major city Wakefield must have been. There are still the remains, just upstream, of the river wharves that made it an important inland port for grain and cloth and, until mills and factories replaced domestic production, it was a far bigger centre for the wool industry than Leeds or Bradford. There are echoes of that old prominence in the city centre, with its cathedral and impressive civic buildings. Like Castleford, it has its representative in sculpture's first division in Barbara Hepworth, whose three bronze figures from a larger group stand in a little square near the Town Hall. You might guess that it would be the exposed rocks and wind-twisted trees of the Pennines that would inspire sculptors, rather than the relatively featureless lowlands of Wakefield and Castleford, but this is Yorkshire's sculpture heartland, a status that is underlined by the array of works in the open air of the Yorkshire Sculpture Park at nearby West Bretton, not far from the National Coalmining Museum, which has to be around here somewhere.

It can be a confusing place, Wakefield. Walking with us through the middle of the city is John Bates, one of Stevo's teammates in the

Dewsbury side which stunned the world – or at least the West Riding of Yorkshire – by winning the Championship in 1973. A lorry driver had an embarrassing moment when he came to a halt to ask directions, only to recognise his boss, John Bates.

* * *

Another thing which Wakefield has going for it is the first serious climb of the walk, the long pull up Lofthouse Hill on the road to Leeds. That presents no problem to Chris. Although Eric seems to lead a fairly sedentary life in *Emmerdale*, his alter-ego is formidably fit. In gaps between filming, he tends to go off to places like Jordan and run three marathons in three days, so a piddling Yorkshire hill does little to slow him down.

Taking it a little more steadily with me at the back is Gary Hetherington, one of the men in rugby league from whom it has been impossible to get away in the last 20 years. As a player, he had stints – not always long ones – with Huddersfield, York, Wigan, Leeds and Hull, but his most lasting legacy was the creation of Sheffield Eagles, partly financed with his earnings from selling windows and conservatories. He cleared off to run Leeds, whilst wife Kath – of the formidable hockey reputation and who once reproached me for something I had written with the unforgettable words: 'You know your trouble? You've been thinking again' – did the same at Gateshead and then at Hull. Between them, they sometimes seem to run half the game from their kitchen table – and a little corner of rugby union as well.

Gary was waiting to hear what the courts were going to do with two of his best young players at the time of our little jaunt, but he also had his hands full with another matter. Considering the number of Sky personnel around, it was not surprising that, when we were not discussing drug scandals and where we might be stopping for the next drink, the topic of the ongoing television negotiations was a popular one. Up at the front, with Stevo, you could hear one version: the Rugby League was playing a dangerous, nay, suicidal game; Rupert Murdoch was about to walk away; Stevo himself had bought his ticket home to Australia and it was – pause for effect – one way.

Further back, Gary was philosophical in the extreme. If Sky cashed in their chips, so be it. There was an offer on the table from the BBC and the game would make up for the shortfall in TV revenue by attracting more people to live games. Internationals needed to be on terrestrial television and the Challenge Cup needed to be moved to later in the year; everyone would be better off with a final in August or September. A hundred yards ahead – where Stevo had decided he must be if he was to win the psychological battle with himself for the rest of the 220 miles – that idea was getting short shrift, along with the Hetherington suggestion that Sky could balance its schedules with live Cup ties. It was a pretty fair summary of the two negotiating positions at the time, although it didn't seem to me that there was much there that was irreconcilable. If you could have got the three parties – League, Sky and BBC – into a room together with some decent wine and a few plates of sandwiches, before pique and injured pride entered into the equation, it should have been possible to sort it all out in a couple of hours. In fact, I occasionally wondered afterwards, during the several months that passed before the issue was resolved, whether we might have been able to do it that day, on the way out of Wakefield, if only we had all been able to walk at the same speed.

Gary was once a bit faster on his feet when it came to raising money for a good cause. Back in 1993, he wanted to sign the Hull and Great Britain hooker, Lee Jackson, for the Eagles, but couldn't afford the asking price. The obvious if demanding solution was a sponsored run from Sheffield to St Helens – 71 miles over three days. 'I was knackered when I finished, but we raised the money for Jacko.' Now, I fear, he would have to walk for 71 days to raise the funds to buy Jacko a new pair of socks in which to play for the York City Knights. As he branches off downhill to Outwood to be picked up by his son and transported to Leeds, I hope that he is right about the TV deal. We have a slower route to the city ahead, crossing – guess what – the M62 near its junction with the M1. From there, we look across to the towering skyline like pilgrims clapping eyes on Jerusalem for the first time.

IV

Leeds: League in its City

THERE WAS A TIME, NOT SO VERY LONG AGO, WHEN LEEDS looked and felt like not much more than a bigger version of other industrial towns in the north of England. Now it feels like a smaller version of London, with different accents, cheaper beer and better scenery. If rugby league in this country has a capital city, this has always been it; now it seems like a powerhouse in a broader sense.

Its rugby league credentials once included three professional clubs – two at the moment, but that could change – and still include countless amateur sides and the League's headquarters, moved here from Oldham in 1920 because it was where its then secretary, John Wilson, lived. The HQ used to be in the (ahem) lively inner-city area of Chapeltown, where it was once said by one member of staff that you could get a joint, a gun, a girl and a Cup final ticket, all by standing in the same queue. It is now miles out on the Wetherby Road; next to a garden centre, so you could buy a few nice shrubs, some potting compost and a Grand Final ticket on one trip. Times change.

Times have changed for the city too, with its Harvey Nichols and its thriving legal and financial sector, but there is rather a lot of Leeds to walk through before you get to boom-town Leeds. Belle Isle might sound like some tropical paradise, but the reality is of a sprawling estate where old men with the shakes – maybe not as old as they look – wait outside the pubs at 11 in the morning. Not far away is the pub where one of Gary Hetherington's former Sheffield Eagles players, David Nelson, was shot dead a couple of years earlier. It is the rugged part of town and rugby league is important here.

We go past Belle Isle's pitch, but the group of lads – out for a ride on their bikes, or possibly on somebody else's – who join us play their rugby at Hunslet Parkside, the famous nursery club just across the way that produced the likes of Garry Schofield and Jason Robinson. They recognise Stevo, of course, but they also seem to be *Emmerdale* fans and they want Chris to be in character. 'C'mon Eric. Give us a bit of Eric, Eric.'

Chris explains patiently, but not, I suspect, for the first time: 'I'm not Eric at the moment. I'm only Eric when I'm being paid to be Eric and, at the moment, nobody's paying me to be Eric.' If only Stevo followed the same guidelines, how much more peaceful a world this would be.

'Go on, Eric. Give us a bit of Eric.' So he gives them what is either a bit of Eric, or a bit of Chris getting thoroughly pissed off.

The sporting geography of Leeds is rather odd. Headingley, with all its depth of rugby league history, is deep in what were once the solidly middle-class suburbs to the north of the city and is now absorbed into student bedsit land, but it is south Leeds that produces the players. Many of them gravitate to Headingley, but, in the good old days, there were always enough to sustain an almost equally powerful club south of the River Aire. At our nearest point, we are only a quarter of a mile from Hunslet's present ground, the South Leeds Stadium, and a little further from their traditional home at Parkside, now covered by an industrial estate. Hunslet were famous for having the most specific colours in rugby league – not merely green, white and amber but myrtle, white and flame – as well as the second-best song, after 'Old Faithful', but I have never met anyone capable of giving me a rendition of 'We've Swept the Seas Before'. It's one of my unfulfilled ambitions in the game – along with seeing Great Britain win the Ashes and playing just one more game in the North West Counties Fifth Division – to hear the massed ranks of Hunslet supporters belting it out whilst waving myrtle and flame scarves; always assuming that it's the sort of song you do belt out, because it could be an introspective dirge for all I know. Hunslet, when they were known as New Hunslet and played at the greyhound stadium on Elland Road, were also famous for their American football-style tuning-fork goalposts. While the fabric of a once-great club was collapsing, the shape of those damned sticks often seemed to be the major issue, but rugby league has always kept things like that in proportion. The club also spent time ground-sharing with Leeds United, who, despite going broke and having to be bailed out by the council buying their ground, always treated that arrangement as a grievous affront and were full of tricks like turning off the hot water on the Sundays when Hunslet were at home. That's why Hunslet were a much dirtier team than that Wakefield Trinity side of the early '60s that spent four days in the bath for its art and why anyone with an ounce of rugby league about them should chuckle unashamedly at Leeds United's current plight.

Bill Moore, an Outward Bound fund-raiser from Wakefield who is walking with us, recalls paying 2s 6d for a Cup final ticket in 1965, when Hunslet lost to Wigan in what was generally considered to be one of the very best matches at Wembley. It was the last time the club really rubbed shoulders with the elite, although they could, in theory, have been promoted to Super League in 1999, when they won their Premiership. The South Leeds Stadium, which is like a sports centre with a rugby pitch tagged on, was, not surprisingly, considered inadequate for Super League. A modernised Parkside, famed for having the best playing surface in the game, would have been just fine. And no, Bill can't remember either the words or the tune to 'We've Swept the Seas Before'.

By the time we've established that, we are sweeping into Leeds proper, passing through the glass-fronted canyons that mark its new prosperity. Apart from the endless office buildings – what do people do in there? – there are the residential blocks where the likes of Gary Connolly own flats, or probably apartments in this price range. Down the little side streets near the river, which just a few years ago were neglected and squalid, there are places where you can pay 30 quid for lunch, although I doubt whether Gary does that.

Our immediate destination is the Queens Hotel, an art deco

masterpiece built into, and originally built to serve, the recently modernised railway station. Stevo points up to the top floor: 'That's where Eddie Waring used to live,' he says. It's a story of which I was vaguely aware: the iconic but increasingly eccentric television commentator – that's Waring not Stevo – secreting himself away for years in a Leeds hotel. I made a mental note to investigate further, some day when I didn't have another eight miles to walk before being let off the leash. As with a number of rugby league myths, the truth, as I have pieced it together since, turns out to be a good deal stranger than the fiction.

As luck would have it, I was due to attend a couple of rugby league functions at the Queens and I wondered whether it might be possible to see the suite of rooms in which I imagined Waring as a recluse, venturing out only once a week to further infuriate anybody who took the game at all seriously, with commentaries so surreal that the dividing line between them and his work on *It's a Knockout* was more and more blurred. The early enquiries were not promising. The first person I asked hadn't heard of Eddie Waring and was only vaguely aware of something called rugby league, but eventually the general manager's PA promised to investigate. She spoke to a few aged retainers who had been there during Waring's broadcasting heyday and they told her that he had never lived there, although he might occasionally have stayed. It could have been a way of fobbing me off; after all, they are unlikely to use the line that the hotel was once home to an increasingly strange rugby league commentator in their publicity and might not even be keen to acknowledge the fact at all.

In fact, the plaque by the door, if they had one, should not read 'Eddie Waring Lived Here' but 'Eddie Waring Pretended to Live Here'. It's a monument to the success of the deception that people still believe it. Apparently, he was so spooked by the hostility towards his knockabout style that he encountered on the rugby league circuit that he adopted the Queens as his accommodation address. All his mail went there; if you wanted to meet him, you had to go there. He actually lived somewhere near Sowerby Bridge, but nobody was quite sure where. Another example of the same paranoia – if paranoia it was, because being paranoid doesn't necessarily mean that people aren't out to get you – was the way he used to sneak in and out of grounds before and after games, trying to avoid any contact with a potentially hostile public. And yet, in parts of the country where rugby league was otherwise unknown, he was part of popular culture, with zany undergraduates forming Eddie Waring Appreciation Societies and fêting him as their hero. Ah, the post-modern irony of it all. In Rugby League Land, you can still start a furious argument about the mistreatment of the game by the media, even among those who can barely have any recollection of him at work, merely by mentioning his name. It is what you might call a mixed legacy and it ignores much that he did to strengthen and popularise the game as a journalist and as secretary-manager of Dewsbury, the home town he had in common with Stevo. There must be something in the water.

Ray French, who eventually took over from him at the BBC, recalls that Waring had a unique contract, under the terms of which he had to be the commentator for as long as the Corporation covered rugby league. He became a victim of his own negotiating coup, because he carried on wielding the microphone long after he was capable of doing the job – thus the need to pretend to live in a hotel in Leeds. Towards the end, he had an offsider with a white glove, who pointed to the name of the player in possession on a huge chart that Waring had in front of him and that, rather than the match, was what he watched. It's the white glove that clinches it, really.

* * *

There are still those who feel nostalgic for the game as it was in Eddie Waring's heyday and one of their main gripes is that 'there's not the characters in the game these days'. Well, the nature of full-time professionalism in Super League is that you don't have players with the hinterland that they once had. By and large, they don't have other jobs, like Geoff Fletcher's pig-farming – not even window-cleaning, which has kept many a player, including even a young Phil Clarke, going through the close-season. Interesting hobbies are a bit thin on the ground as well; the television time accorded to pigeon-fancying alone in Waring's commentaries would have paid for a few weeks at the Queens. But anyone who says there are no characters any more has never met Barrie McDermott.

Barrie Mac, as he is generally known, is responsible for some of the most horrible acts I've seen on a rugby field in recent years. Although he has had his moments off it as well, the Law of Inverse Virtue definitely applies in his case. That law states that it is the hardest and nastiest players who are the most likeable blokes in real life – and the most likely to meet you outside the Queens and walk a few miles with you. Phil had written to every living Great Britain international inviting them to do so and the response had disappointed him, although there was a poignancy when someone like the old Warrington second-rower, Jim Featherstone, who won the last of his six caps in 1952 and must be around 80, wrote back to say that he was afraid he couldn't walk very far any more. One very illustrious player of more recent vintage told a star-struck young Adam, one of our back-up team, when he approached him for an autograph at Headingley, that he certainly wouldn't be joining us, as he considered it nothing more than a publicity stunt. I'd tell you who it was, but I don't want to give him the publicity. There were some of the current generation who we knew we could rely on and McDermott, despite or perhaps because of his blood-curdling reputation, was just about top of that list.

Barrie's philosophy on the field can be summed up by something he said when he emceed a night for us in the Supporters' Club at Headingley during the Trek – and did it with great panache.

'I don't know anything about rules,' he said. 'All I know is that, if they show you a yellow card, you're going off for a while. If they show you a red card, you're going off and you're not coming back. And, if they show the other bloke a green card with a cross on it, you're doing your job all right.' Coaching manuals, who needs them?

Barrie has had what could safely be called a colourful history. He lost an eye in a boyhood accident. He was the first person in Britain – not merely the first rugby league player, mind – to be subdued by the police using CS gas, something that has given him a particular empathy with younger players who have got themselves into even worse trouble on nights out. He was shown the door at Wigan, largely because of his indiscipline, and has been involved in some of the scariest on-field moments in the modern era – notably with his Great Britain teammate, but opponent at club level, Stuart Fielden.

He has also successfully reinvented himself as something of an elder statesman, a Renaissance Man of the game. He is a thoughtful magazine columnist and is writing his life story. He is also one of a little group of senior players – Dean Sampson and Brad Davis are two others – to emerge as an articulate analyst of the game for radio and TV. We might never get to the state of rugby union and cricket, where ex-players heavily outnumber journalists – and a damn good thing if we don't, says my bank manager – but it is to rugby league's benefit to have a few who can turn their hand to this sort of thing, rather than just mumbling in embarrassment. He could also make a living as a stand-up comedian or as an after-dinner speaker. One thing I imagine he likes about any of these jobs is that they don't let you get warmed up for 15 minutes and then bring a substitute on. He is a prop forward of the old school and one of the few players, along with Bobby/Bobbie Goulding, to change the spelling of his name in mid-career.

On a training day, Barrie drives over from Oldham with Kevin Sinfield. There used to be another lad named Iestyn Harris with them on that regular M62 shuttle run, but he missed his lift one day and hasn't been heard of since. I wonder what happened to him?

If Barrie Mac is an inheritor of the old, larger-than-life tradition that goes with his role in the game, then Kevin Sinfield is the epitome of rugby league in the twenty-first century – polite, earnest, serious, the product of a time when the sport became a full-time occupation. It is no accident that as soon as he arrives outside the Queens he is deep in conversation with the Great Britain coach, David Waite. Here are two men of different generations whose earnestness makes them a perfect match. Another, more irreverent, Great Britain international recently admitted to me that he still understood very little of what Waite had ever said to him; Kevin would never say such a thing. He is hanging on every word, eager for any information even during his time off. That's the sort of character he is and the reason, as much as his great ability, why coaches will always love him.

David Waite is an Australian, which means that the whole idea of appointing him as Great Britain coach was inevitably a controversial one, even though this is a Rubicon which has been crossed and re-crossed in most other sports. What no one can dispute is that he knows his stuff. To hear him dissecting the strengths and weaknesses of a player is a genuine education. When he goes into coach-speak, however, you can write three pages of notes and finish with half a quotable sentence; and, although it must be partly my fault as well, I've always found that attempts at small-talk with him have been doomed to failure.

There was the time when a few of us went for a post-match pint in the Gaping Goose at Wibsey, not far from Odsal. As I was ordering at the bar, David came in and I asked him what he would have. When he decided on a pint of Taylor's Landlord, I congratulated him on the soundness of his choice, especially as it was a product which had recently received a glowing endorsement from a well-known real ale connoisseur.

'Madonna drinks that, you know,' I told him.

'Does he?'

'Er, no . . . Madonna, the singer. The female singer.'

'Oh, I thought you said your dad drinks it.'

As it happens, he does drink it. But, do you know, Timothy Taylor and Co. of Keighley have never really used that in their advertising, any more than the Queens Hotel have with Eddie Waring. As I say, it's probably my fault, but that exchange in the Gaping Goose remains the most coherent dialogue we've ever had.

* * *

Across City Square from the Queens as we launch our balloons and get under way once more is the nightclub that was the scene of the Lee Bowyer/Jonathan Woodgate fracas that kept lawyers going for some time. The one that figured in the case that saw three Leeds rugby players, plus one from Rochdale, hauled before the courts is a little further away. The club – and the game in general – was waiting for the verdicts whilst we were in Leeds and as we walked out of the city centre, past the former headquarters of Super League (Europe) in the days when it was a rival government of the game, and up Kirkstall Lane, the silhouette of Armley Jail on the skyline was a reminder that those four were by no means the first to feel the wrath of the law. Had we veered right, we would have been on our way to Headingley, but we had already spent a couple of evenings there and further detours were considered unnecessary.

Headingley is now a ground for all seasons and for all tastes. Apart from the long-established cricket and rugby league, it is now also home to the Leeds Tykes rugby union side. To many of us, that felt akin to betrayal. After all, in the battle for hearts and minds in the north of England, one of the strengths of rugby league is that rugby union has traditionally been weak. So giving them a foothold at Headingley just seemed a bad idea in a strategic sense. Leeds proudly head their letters with 'The World's First Rugby Partnership'. To me, that's the equivalent of finding this inscription on the fabled Wooden Horse: 'The World's First Greek–Trojan Joint Venture'.

When the plan was announced, Gary Hetherington said something truly shocking: that it would give Leeds supporters some rugby to watch in the winter, conveniently ignoring the way that all amateur rugby league and much professional league outside Super League was played at that time of year. Leeds supporters have not embraced the Tykes; when there has been an attempt to double-head the two codes, I have never seen so many people with their backs to the pitch, and a firm called Southstander – as in the South Stand at Headingley – makes and sells a range of goods bearing the logo '100% League. 0% Union'. The financial reality is, however, that Leeds were rescued from meltdown by Paul Caddick, a Castleford-based millionaire whose game is union, so ideological purity was not an option. The Tykes have their own audience, largely from out of town and from those fancy downtown apartments, but some as well from the northern suburbs that never were rock-solid league territory. When a mate of mine set up a team called North Leeds, it almost counted as a development area. There has also been some limited interchange of players, with Liam Botham, whose dad achieved a bit of success at Headingley, actually making his debut for the Rhinos before he did for the Tykes. But, with my '100% League' hat on, it still feels all wrong.

Just as Leeds is rugby league's home city, so Headingley is its home ground. Even the cricket ground is rugby league territory, because one Christmas, when the rugby ground was frozen solid, they switched the game to the other side of the stand. One man with a keen appreciation of this depth of tradition is Stephen Ball, Headingley's stadium manager and former chairman of Batley. In that previous role, he was the man who once gave the team the bonus of a box of biscuits each for a particularly good win. That prompted the question of what the incentive would be if they could keep up the good work next time out. 'Well, it's Christmas soon,' he mused. 'We could be talking turkey.' Unlike some at Headingley, Ball doesn't make much pretence of being interested in the union adventure; league is his game and he wants the place to be even more closely tied into its history and culture.

One of the scandals of the game is that it has nowhere to show off the relics and artefacts of its past. There used to be a pub at Oulton, on the outskirts of Leeds, that housed the Rugby League Hall of Fame, but, when Whitbread's sponsorship ended and the pub adopted a different theme, all the material on display there was packed away in cardboard boxes. Worse still, when the League moved from Chapeltown, scavengers found priceless memorabilia, like old tour photos and international caps, dumped in skips around the back. You couldn't find a better illustration of rugby league's cavalier disregard for its own history. The administration at the time failed to mark the game's centenary in 1995 with anything like the enthusiasm it deserved. It didn't help that it was the year that Super League reared its head; there were too many people around who thought they were inventing the game there and then.

There has been talk of a museum in Huddersfield, the birthplace of the code, and in Widnes, where Halton Council announced, at one optimistic stage, that they were rescuing the twin towers from the demolition site that was Wembley Stadium and re-erecting them on the banks of the Mersey. It would have made a nice end for the Trek, but the scepticism that greeted that ambitious scheme proved all too prescient. Ironically, the only proper display devoted to rugby league's history is at Twickenham (insert several exclamation marks here) where one room of their museum is devoted to the rebels.

Stephen Ball would like to change all this by creating a museum at Headingley and it is hard to argue with his contention that it would be the ideal setting, at the closest thing the game has to a headquarters. You could even devote a room to rugby union and its connections with our code. Steve doesn't want to stop there, because he has a bee in his bonnet about giving his game a platform. His other scheme is for a statue, symbolising rugby league in some way, to be erected somewhere along the M62 – where else? It might sound fanciful, but that's what they said about The Angel of the North and it would be a dull and miserable Geordie, or a dull and miserable visitor from anywhere else, whose heart didn't lift when he or she saw that. If people saw something comparable as they crossed the Pennines and were told that it was The Spirit of Rugby League, the exercise would surely be worthwhile. When I spoke to Steve, he was investigating a couple of possible sites, but I have an idea of my own. More of that later, because we aren't meant to be at Headingley at all, and I didn't even have time for a sentimental look at the single-track bridge that leads to the ground from Burley, where the Blackpool Borough coach – the vehicle, not the person – got stuck on 23 March 1980. They legged it to the changing-rooms just in time, played in borrowed jockstraps and won. No, no time to dwell on that, no time even to mention it, because we are on our way to a very different part of Leeds.

* * *

There is another rugby league heartland in the city, apart from Hunslet; it is in west Leeds and doesn't quite have the same glamour. Our expanding party – with Ken back with us, as well as several new families from Leeds and the Rhinos contingent led by Barrie Mac – gets there by turning left, down the dip and over the River Aire and the Leeds–Liverpool Canal, then up the hill on the other side. This is Armley, famed for the aforementioned jail, but also home to what look like Leeds' most depressing tower blocks. There is a new dual carriageway, but the old route, down Town Street towards Bramley, is a bustling cityscape I'd never seen before. It was a grey old day by this stage, but there was a colour and life about the place you couldn't help but like.

Unlike Hunslet, Bramley were never a successful club, although they had their moment of glory in 1973–74, when they won the BBC2 Floodlit Trophy by beating Widnes – in broad daylight, because of the restrictions on electricity use during the so-called Three Day Week. Apart from that, life was pretty much one long struggle, with the biggest thing that happened to the club its sideways shuffle from its old ground – the Barley Mow, named after the adjacent pub – to McLaren Field. They were close enough that gardens of houses next to the latter contained the remains of floodlight pylons – appropriate really – from the original. One of them had roses growing up it, as I recall. McLaren Field is now covered by houses as well, some of them with floodlit gazebos in the back gardens, for all I know.

In a peculiar twist of events, even by rugby league standards, Bramley finished up at Headingley, playing as what amounted to Leeds' second team. If you had a real stinker, you could find yourself playing on the same ground as usual, but for a very different team. The roster for the 1998 season includes such luminaries as Terry Newton, Dean Lawford, Leroy Rivett and – yes – Barrie McDermott. I wonder if that will be in his book; not a whole chapter, I bet.

There were a few quirks that made Bramley's sojourn at Headingley unforgettable. Instead of the customary 64-page programme, they used to produce a handwritten team-sheet, on which the surnames were always listed first. One night, Lancashire Lynx – who were the successors to Blackpool Borough, sort of – had Neil Parsley and Neil Allday in their team, or rather they had Parsley Neil and Allday Neil. 'These Neil lads,' someone asked in the press box. 'Are they related?' Rum names in Lancashire.

West Leeds lost its professional club when Bramley were kicked out of the League for the 2000 season, but its hard core of supporters, and especially the Spracklen family, have never given up the ghost. They tried and failed to get back in, ground-sharing with Farsley Celtic. As we walked up past the former sites of McLaren Field and the Barley Mow, they were working away at a new application to a new competition – National League Three. It's essentially an amateur league and it might never lead any higher, but it represents a continued presence for a long-established club. Bramley Buffaloes, if they get the go-ahead, will play at Stanningley, the next place up the road, where the existing amateur club has tapped into some hefty grant aid to improve its ground. A club with a famous name playing there in the summer, just a few hundred yards from its traditional home, would restore the rugby league equilibrium of the city. And just watch out for them if we ever have another Miners' Strike and Three Day Week – unlikely, unless the staff of the National Coalmining Museum bring the country to its knees by downing tools.

As we go through Stanningley and up the hill towards New Pudsey, the drizzle getting heavier as we go, there's an 'Eh up!' and a familiar, grizzled face on the other side of a fence. Throwing lumps of metal around in a scrapyard is the unmistakable figure of Roy Dickinson, a cheerful and willing prop forward for Leeds and Halifax in the '70s and '80s and the coach of Bramley for a couple of seasons. The last time I'd seen him was on the Isle of Man for one of the Charity Shield matches over there, enjoying a pint in a harbour-side pub in Douglas. He wasn't playing or anything, he just fancied the trip. Where will it be next time? On top of Snowdon? In a karaoke bar in Tokyo? We will probably resume the same casual chat about the state of the game. Rugby league is like that, whether it has a museum and a statue to call its own or not.

V

Bradford:
The Bull in this Place Goes on Forever

THERE ISN'T ANY BREATHING SPACE BETWEEN LEEDS AND
Bradford these days. There hasn't been for some time. In fact, there
can't be two comparable cities in Britain as claustrophobically close
to each other; not if you don't count Manchester and Salford, which
are a bit of a special case. J.B. Priestley, a Bradford man, had a theory
about their relationship. Bradford, he reckoned, lost out because the
main railway lines ran through Leeds, 'with the result that Leeds,
though it has never had the world-wide reputation of Bradford, is a
larger city and of much greater local importance'. Even now, the
rivalry between the two cities goes way beyond the sporting arena,
but it is only in sport – and, arguably, only in rugby league – that it
is a level playing field. No wonder that derbies between the Bulls
and the Rhinos carry a special charge; one that many now feel makes
them bigger events than those between Wigan and St Helens. There
was a nice moment on Radio Five recently, when the link-man in the
studio in London spoke to a match commentator at Elland Road and
said that he supposed the back page of the *Yorkshire Post* would be
full of speculation over whether Peter Reid would keep his job, that
being the Leeds United drama at the time. On the contrary, he was
told, it was full of the build-up to Leeds and Bradford's fifth clash
of the season. Fifth, mind; you can't even argue that it had much

novelty value, but it was undeniably the big story.

In the 1800s, two-thirds of Britain's wool production went through Bradford. A key factor in Priestley's contention that it was, and remained for a long time, a bigger player on the world stage than Leeds, was the presence in the city of large numbers of German-Jewish merchants. Their influence is now only detectable in a sprinkling of Germanic surnames and the distinctive architecture of Little Germany, the old commercial area we skirt on our way to the city centre. These days, Bradford is known, even to those who have never been near the place, for a different wave of immigration and a different set of influences.

It is, at least in parts, the most obviously Asian city in Britain and must have more Asian businesses and Indian restaurants – even if that is almost always a misnomer – than anywhere of similar size. You can eat like a king in establishments that resemble Mogul palaces, but without the same sense of decorative restraint – as we did one night. The best food, though, is often in the simplest places, preferably with no tablecloths or cutlery, where you scoop it up with chapattis. You can go on packaged Curry Weekends to Bradford and sample both ends of the scale without straying very far from Little Horton Lane. Another heavily Asian area is Manningham, the scene of prolonged racial violence in 2002, when the Bulls were in temporary residence at Bradford City's ground, Valley Parade. I rather liked the cosmopolitan surroundings – there was certainly a much more rewarding choice of food and drink in Manningham than the one pub and one chippy in adjoining Odsal – but I was in the minority. Rugby fans never warmed to Valley Parade and the fact that it was in an area which they had seen burst into flames on their TVs did not help.

From New Pudsey Station, an unofficial staging post between Leeds and Bradford, we are accompanied by a gaggle of youngsters – most but not all of them Asian – who have been involved in Outward Bound courses. Going through Thornbury and Laisterdyke towards the city centre, their local knowledge proves invaluable, because they know which local businesses to chivvy for contributions to the cause.

One thing they can do nothing about is the weather, which has taken on the appearance of a sub-continental monsoon. So far on the Trek, we had been lucky. It had been bright, breezy, not too hot, with only the occasional shower. Perfect walking weather, in fact, but Bradford was making up for it and had been doing so since first footfall.

Some people don't mind walking in the rain. Some even prefer it. I've done plenty of it – I come from the north of England, for heaven's sake – but I hate it more and more. Alfred Wainwright hiked the Lakeland Fells, the Peak District and the Scottish Mountains in nothing more water-resistant than a Harris tweed jacket. Nowadays we have the full range of all-weather garments made out of high-tech fabrics that always have an X in them, which are supposed to keep the rain out and send the sweat out to join it. I've invested in a few of these miraculous vestments in my time, of all manner of fancy brands, and the result has always been the same. They hoard every precious bead of perspiration like misers with silver sixpences and suck in every vaguely adjacent droplet from the outside world to top up the liquid level within. Could it be, I've wondered on occasion, that I've been wearing them all inside-out? In my experience, breathable waterproof clothing is as cruel a confidence trick as pyramid selling and chain letters.

So it was understandable that I was looking forward to road-testing the latest in the long line of jackets that promised to keep me dry – a very snazzy-looking item kindly donated by a generous supporter of the Trek. This, after a lifetime of disappointments, could really be the one, but this was the point at which Irish Phil intervened.

'Don't be messing around with that,' he said. 'This is the one you need. Cost £250, guaranteed completely waterproof! Breathable! Sure, I'll be in the camper van keeping dry, but you've got to use it. Believe me, it's the business.'

Fragile as he was from the night before and insistent as he was that he had the answer, it seemed rude to refuse. That was why, minutes later, I was trudging towards Bradford, soaked to the skin, wearing something that felt like a parachute that had been ditched in the North Sea. Of all the drenchings I have had, courtesy of the high-performance outerwear industry, this was the most comprehensive. It was as effective as wearing a suit made out of sponge. The only time I've been nearly as wet in this country was when I was a cub reporter in Shropshire and rode through a deluge on my motorbike to the one-man office at Whitchurch. The only thing to do was to take everything off and dry it in front of the electric fire, whilst I sat naked, tapping away at the upright typewriter. Unfortunately, I neglected to lock the door and it was a bit of a shock for Mrs Carruthers from the Women's Institute when she brought in the results from the produce show.

'Ah now,' says Phil later, with the air of a man suddenly remembering something. 'I was still a bit pissed this morning. It could be windproof that it's supposed to be.'

For the first time, I was seriously questioning whether this had all been such a good idea. I had met Suzie, Outward Bound's corporate projects manager, and she looked like Ulrika Jonsson before she started getting knocked around by footballers. Surely it would be simpler and more effective – not to mention drier – to send her out to approach people, smile sweetly and ask them to give her all their money. I can't imagine anyone refusing and we could have all stayed indoors, drinking hot chocolate and playing Scrabble in front of a roaring fire.

* * *

Even peering between the stair-rods, you can detect that there is something different about Bradford. Unlike Leeds, all the impressive stuff is the old stuff, like the classical frontage of St George's Hall, the ornate Alhambra Theatre and the Victorian high Gothic of the City Hall, with its Florentine-inspired clock tower. That was where we were bound, for the most glittering occasion so far – although pizza in Ray Tennant's backyard came close. The mayor had invited us to a civic reception and although a bereavement prevented his own attendance, his deputy had been busy buttering the finger rolls and quartering the whist pies. Best of all, this all took place in a room with a roof.

Outward Bound in Bradford alone provides 2,000 bursaries a year, sending young people from all backgrounds on courses in the great outdoors. A succession of those young people made affecting little speeches about how tongue-tied and lacking in confidence they had been before that experience. If they were that way before, they certainly aren't now; a little damp maybe, but not short of confidence. The backdrop is the illuminated panel that lists Bradford's lord mayors, resonant names that tell of a legacy of civic solidity as concisely as the headstones at the nearby Undercliffe Cemetery, one of Europe's biggest and grandest: Manoah Rhodes (1873–4); Herbert Hustler Tetley (1918); and Meredith Farrar Titterington, who saw them through that tricky period from 1939 to 1940.

Named and pictured in an adjacent chamber is one of Bradford's favourite adopted sons, the remarkable Trevor Foster. He 'Came North', as the Welsh put it, from Newport in 1938, when Meredith Farrar Titterington – a bit of Welsh there, I wonder – was a mere up-and-coming alderman. He became one of the best second-rowers of his era, playing 462 games before retiring in 1955. Retiring is the wrong word for Trevor, though, because he has been active ever since in providing sporting opportunities for young Bradfordians at the Police Boys' Club. He is still the official timekeeper at Odsal and, if anyone deserves credit for the game finally taking its showpiece, the Challenge Cup final, to Cardiff, he is the man, because he campaigned persuasively for that for years. Trevor is one of those we knew would turn up to meet us; his opinion of the project is summed up in a word he uses often: 'Marvellous, marvellous.' Other old-timers – and not so old-timers – make an art-form of moaning about everything in the modern world and especially everything in the game, but to Trevor it's all 'marvellous'. At 87, he is still as fit as a flea and he wants to walk with us, but he hasn't brought his raincoat and we talk him out of it. Unfortunately for Robbie Paul and Stuart Fielden – a pair of blue-chip injured players, if ever we had them – we are accepting no such excuses from them.

Turning left at Jacob's Well and up Manchester Road, the snappily named National Museum of Photography, Film and Television is on our right. It has a particular place in my affections, because it was here that Super League held a pre-season launch which Ellery Hanley – a Leeds man, but a Bradford hero – refused to attend and was ultimately sacked as coach of St Helens. That same day, there was an exhibition in the museum of the work of David Hockney – another Bradford hero. Hanley and Hockney . . . what a combination. Others upon whom the Metropolitan District has a claim are the Brontë sisters, born in Thornton, a couple of miles to the west of the city centre, but more often associated with Haworth, where they amount to a local industry. If there had been a decent amateur rugby league club in the area at the time, I feel sure that their brother, Bramwell, would not have gone to the bad the way he did.

Stuart Fielden, as I know Trevor feels, is a marvel of the modern game. He has all the agility and mobility you could ask for from a twenty-first-century rugby league forward, but he would love to play, like the old-timers did and he is allowed to sometimes, for the full 80 minutes. That should take a terrible toll on the body and he is indeed recovering from minor surgery and giving his knee a bit of a test drive up Manchester Road. It is Robbie Paul, though, who epitomises everything that has happened to rugby league in Bradford over the last few years.

Robbie is what the late Peter Deakin used to call 'a franchise player' – a phrase borrowed from his time studying the way they do things in American sport. By that he meant a player whose image, whose personality, becomes synonymous with the club. That has certainly happened with Robbie at Bradford, since he arrived there from New Zealand as a little-known teenager in 1994. He is not only a dazzling, individualistic player, he can talk the hind legs off a donkey on just about any subject and he is an accomplished artist, with a studio above an Indian takeaway. When Bradford signed his elder brother, Henry, they started putting 'Robbie' on the back of his shirt, rather than his surname, in order to distinguish the two. Now Henry has gone, Robbie is still Robbie.

All this has been going on against the backdrop of the complete transformation of what used to be called Bradford Northern, or sometimes the Steam Pigs, with its suggestion of hard, mechanical labour. In many ways, Northern were unlikely candidates for leading the way in this process of reinvention. It was not that they were complete strangers to success; they had been to Wembley three times in three years in Trevor Foster's day after the Second World

War and they twice won the First Division Championship at the start of the '80s under the coaching of Peter Fox. An official crowd of 102,569 watched the Challenge Cup final replay between Warrington and Halifax at Odsal in 1954, with traffic jams, in those pre-M62 days, stretching back over the Pennines to Oldham. The historian Robert Gate's book on the event is cogently entitled *There Were a Lot More There Than That* – but, far more often, crowds were lost in the vastness of Odsal's bowl like a single sock in a spin-drier. Even Fox's Championship-winners were watched by average home gates of little more than 6,000. Northern, even when they were winning, seemed grim. Deakin, with his ideas from America, Australia and, lest we forget, from Keighley, where in the north of the Metropolitan District of Bradford Cougarmania had played the John the Baptist role, turned them into an all-singing, all-dancing, three-ring circus.

I didn't like everything about his style of match-day presentation. Much of it seemed crass in the extreme, but it wasn't aimed at people like me, who would be going to the match anyway. More traditional fans in places like Halifax still take the mickey out of the keep-the-kiddies-happy ethos of the place these days, but they would surely love to capture the same enthusiasm at their own grounds. It is all the more remarkable that this has all taken place under the chairmanship of Chris Caisley, the most grim-faced and permanently disgruntled man in the game. It's a little like putting Scrooge in charge of the kiddies' Christmas party, but, for some mysterious reason, it has worked.

The showmanship of Odsal has produced some memorable moments, like the time when what seemed like hundreds of Hell's Angels appeared on the lip of the bowl on their bikes, silhouetted against the sunset. If they looked menacing, someone suggested, it was because they had come for the money they were due for their first appearance. I also like to think that the constant use of Sam the Sham and the Pharaohs' 1965 hit, 'Woolly Bully', is a reference to Bradford's importance in the worsted industry, but I could be reading too much into that.

It's hard to remember now what a furore it caused when Bradford dropped the Northern from their name and replaced it with Bulls.

To many it seemed like vandalism or the betrayal of a heritage, but, as a marketing ploy, it was triumphant. I have a rule of thumb about when it is valid to refer to a club by its newfangled nickname. It is when you can go to a neighbouring town or city and call them by that name and be clearly understood. Leeds Rhinos have just about got there; Wigan Warriors are nowhere near; and the Halifax Blue Sox never had a chance. The Bulls, with flair and novelty on their side, got there almost immediately.

The great thing about Robbie Paul, who was actually signed by Peter Fox and so straddles the two eras, is the irresistible impression he gives of having enjoyed every minute of it, on and off the pitch. If he enjoyed the 2003 season less than most, it was because he spent the latter stages of it convalescing from a triple break of his arm. In his desperation to speed his recovery, he was preparing, as we walked up Manchester Road, to fly to the Isle of Man at his own expense to put himself under pressure in an especially good hyperbaric chamber they have over there. That is the cue for an excellent rainy-day story from Phil Clarke, about a teammate of his – who had better remain nameless – who found himself sharing such a chamber with a very attractive lady javelin champion. He emerged to boast of joining a club far more exclusive than the Mile High Club, one that should perhaps be known henceforth as the Mile Deep Club.

* * *

This was also the day when two Leeds players joined a rather less exclusive club – that reserved for players who have been sent to jail, or to a young offenders' institution, to be strictly accurate in this case. For their parts in a brawl outside a nightclub, Chev Walker was sent down for eighteen months and Ryan Bailey for nine. These were not obscure players; despite their youth, both were members of David Waite's Great Britain squad preparing for the arrival of the Australians, as well as being key members of the Leeds squad. It was another good day not to be working, as a wave of moral panic swept through the game. Phil Clarke, with his GB manager's hat on, was mentally crossing a couple of names off his team-sheet, as Leeds declared that they would be standing by their men. That was what you would expect, but the unworthy thought crossed my mind that they might have taken a slightly different view if they had been a couple of obscure reserves or a pair of clapped-out veterans. Given the depth of rivalry between the two clubs and the two cities, there was what might have seemed a surprising lack of gloating about all this in Bradford. There was a reason for that: one of the Bulls' best young players – and current Great Britain international – Leon Pryce, had similar charges arising out of similar circumstances hanging over his head. Three international-class players in court for offences of violence – it pales a little alongside some of the things that have happened in football of late, but it still sits uncomfortably with the family-game image that rugby league cultivates so carefully. To encourage young men to entertain those families, we maximise their strength and aggression, pay them a good deal of money and turn them loose in city centres, with all their temptations and provocations. It should be no surprise that it occasionally goes pear-shaped.

* * *

The Bulls, as you would expect, have thrown themselves into the venture with their customary enthusiasm, organising a Family Fun Day to coincide with our arrival at Odsal. Despite the filthy weather, there's a little crowd assembled outside the Top House and a pint on the bar for anyone who's made it from Hull. Across the road, one of the Trek's lump-in-the-throat moments awaits as we are played into the stadium by Pipe Sgt Iain Hutton of the Royal Dragoon Guards. A much maligned instrument, the bagpipes, they are only heard at their best outdoors and, preferably, in driving rain. There were people there who deserved that uplifting welcome more than us; the mums and dads who'd promised their offspring a day out at Odsal and were damn well going to give them one, whatever the weather; and, most of all, the select group of Rhinos' fans who had set off with us from the Queens, 24 hours earlier. I presume they went home from New Pudsey and came back the following morning to resume, but I never actually checked. I think they had only intended to come a couple of miles and just got rather carried away with it all.

There is quite a party going on at Odsal, with a climbing-wall, a DJ, the inevitable face-painting. The Bulls can get more people out for something like this, even on this sort of day, than most National League clubs can for a match. Part of that is down to the way they have taken Odsal, a handicap in a winter season, and turned it into their biggest asset. Our day there was a good one to remember just what it could be like in November or January. Odsal, hollowed out of an old rubbish dump, has its own micro-climate. It can be five degrees colder than at street level, or the sun can be shining outside and the stadium can be buried in clouds. I remember one game when a bank of dense fog came rolling in from Rooley Avenue and flopped over the perimeter wall like a fat man collapsing wearily into a bath after, say, walking from Hull. It tumbled down the terracing and lay there contented on the pitch, so that you could see across to the crowd on the opposite side of the stadium as clear as day, but of the action on the pitch, nothing. As soon as the match was abandoned and its job was done, it crawled off over the stock-car pits and slunk off to leave Odsal in the sunshine before the players had even changed into their street clothes. The elements have a mind of their own in these parts.

As I looked down onto the pitch far below, from the spot where the old players used to descend a precarious staircase, running the famous gauntlet of old ladies with bricks in their handbags and sharpened umbrellas, I was reminded of another peculiarity of the place. It is from this angle that you really notice the pitch's odd, curled-up corners. They are a legacy of the stadium's old role as a speedway and stock-car venue and used to be picked up in trays and stashed away when the track was in use. They were a feature of the landscape used expertly by Deryck Fox (no relation) when he had the knack of kicking for the corners and then regathering the ball as it bounced back towards him. It was a party trick made all the more effective if there was a bit of fog around. The club's trick, under Deakin and Gary Tasker and since, has been to turn every match-day into a party, with no part of the stadium wasted. If you have an empty expanse of concrete, stick a bouncy castle on it. That could be their motto.

If there is one disappointment for the club it is that their crowds do not yet reflect the ethnic diversity of the city. On match-days or at gatherings like ours, the Asian population is severely under-represented. It is not for want of trying. The club goes out evangelising in schools which are predominantly Asian, just as it does in ones which are overwhelmingly white, that sort of split often being par for the course in Bradford. When I've been to watch the Bradford variant of touch rugby, called Bull Tag, Asian boys and girls seem to enjoy it every bit as much as whites and I find it hard to imagine that there would be any hostility to them if they were on the terraces in greater numbers, as there is known to be at some football clubs. Bradford Council employs Ikram Butt, the former Featherstone, London Broncos and England winger, to engage Asian youngsters in sport and he works closely with the Bulls, but, for all their efforts, the numbers who actually go to matches remain stubbornly low. Perhaps it needs a few more role models. There are some, like Butt, Junaid Malik from nearby Elland, who captained the Great Britain amateur side, and, one day perhaps, Saqib Murtza, a young prop trying to establish himself in the club's Junior Academy side. It is not a matter which rugby league clubs can afford to neglect, given the demographics of many of the towns and cities in which it is played. Some grounds are surrounded by Asian residential areas; Halifax's old ground at Thrum Hall is an example, as is another of Butt's former clubs, Batley. At some clubs, the temptation is strong to drop-kick it into the too-hard basket. They will tell you that Muslims are not interested in playing highly physical team-sports and not much interested in watching them either. They used to say something very similar in Sydney about the Lebanese immigrants who poured into the city's inner suburbs. Now there are Lebanese players everywhere, including the Lebanon, where the seeds have been sown by Lebanese who learned the game in Australia, and clubs like Canterbury have strong support from the Lebanese community. Ikram Butt runs an occasional team called the South Asia Bulls, whose battle honours include the York International Nines and the All-India Games in Bombay. If they are to be the standard-bearers, it is a very important standard that they bear. And it is a fair bet that if any club breaks through the racial divide, it will be Bradford, because they will continue to work at it.

* * *

After an hour or two at Odsal, where the clouds were now so low that they were halfway down the best seats, we were suffering from an excess of two elements – rain and enthusiasm. The antidote for both was waiting down the road at our hotel for the night. There are few things that feel better after a good soaking than a good soak in a jacuzzi, even though that involved sharing with the not inconsiderable frame of the Bulls' winger, Tevita Vaikona, who was there to unwind. In his days in New Zealand, he will have experienced many dousings in the hot, sulphurous springs that make the whole of Rotorua, for instance, smell like rotten eggs. This, we agree, isn't quite as good as that, but it will do to be going on with.

The other occupant is an elderly chap, with skin wrinkled like a walnut, perhaps from a constant round of immersion in the hot-tub and baking in the sauna and steam-room, because he seems almost to live in the hotel's spa. One place he won't be venturing out to visit is Odsal, because he hates everything about it these days – the kids, the noise, even the rugby. He used to watch in the good old days of flat caps and Bradford Northern, but he hasn't been for years. 'It's not rugby now,' he says. 'It's a load of crap. No skill, nothing. I wouldn't cross the road to watch it now. Bradford Bullshit, I call it.

'Now, the Wigan–Hunslet Cup final in 1965. That was a proper game. They don't make them like that any more.'

This particular match and its place in rugby league folklore is something that Phil Clarke knows a bit about, for good family reasons, and he can't resist the bait.

'Well, my dad played in that match and HE says that THAT was a load of crap. He watched it on video last week and he said he was embarrassed by how slow and useless it was.' But The Walnut isn't listening; he's bobbing off towards the deep end.

There was something almost heroic about his determination to be a miserable old git, but the hotel also yielded someone who was one of the undisputed heroes of the trip. Russell was the local chiropodist we had organised to carry out some running repairs. Amongst his other clients, he worked for Bradford City and Halifax Town, so he was used to dealing with feet rather more valuable than ours – although perhaps not much more valuable in Halifax's case. With his sharp blades and surgical spirit, he dealt ruthlessly with any blisters, most of them on Stevo's feet, where he boasted of having blisters on blisters. My own feet had not been a thing of beauty since an ill-advised and ill-fitting pair of winklepickers in the early '60s, but Russell did his best with the unpromising raw material, taking his chain-saw to the nails and his scalpel to my big toes, whittling off enough translucent shavings of dead skin to re-equip the entire hotel with new lampshades. Apart from considerably lightening my load with that operation, his visit gave me a chance to scrape the calluses off my favourite rugby league chiropodist story – in fact, my only rugby league chiropodist story.

Danny McAllister, an Australian prop and, despite this tale, no fool, was playing for Sheffield Eagles when he visited a practitioner. He told him to remove his socks and shoes and poked around for a while.

'How does that feel?' he asked him.

'Fine,' he replied. 'But how's it going to help my neck?'

'Your neck?'

'Yeah, the club told me to see a chiropractor about my neck and I thought a chiropodist must be the same thing.'

Maybe it's the power of suggestion, but, really and truly, my neck did feel better after Russell's ministrations, so there could be something in the McAllister Theory after all. What's more, he donated his services for free, as his contribution to the Trek. A true hero. In the unlikely event of Bradford City or Halifax Town achieving anything of note, I bet it's down to his good work.

* * *

My feet got some more special treatment that same evening. Standing up and trying to stay awake in a trendy bar back in Headingley after that night's match, I dropped a whole pint over them. It was a luxurious, top-of-the-range foot-bath, because that pint – admittedly of something strong, cloudy and Belgian – had cost me £3.20. By the time I had splodged back to the bar and bitterly bought a replacement and been fined by the kangaroo court convened by Stevo to punish me for the heinous crime of spilling beer – always a no-no on tour – it had cost me £11.40. I told you that Leeds was turning into London; but Bradford remains unmistakably Bradford.

VI

Halifax and Hell

There is an old Yorkshire song called 'The Dalesman's Litany', to which the cheery refrain runs like this:

> From Hull and Halifax and Hell,
> Good Lord, deliver me.

Hull, Halifax and Hell . . . it sounds like a particularly demanding sequence of away games. The song is actually about the horrors of the Industrial Revolution, as seen through the eyes of a country-dweller, and it was more than mere alliteration that led him to bracket the three places together.

Well, we've been to Hull and it didn't seem particularly hellish, although it might have done had you been a dalesman suddenly dropped into its narrow backstreets in mid-Victorian times. Halifax, perhaps because we were there intruding into the private grief that was the 2003 season, can sometimes wear an altogether more infernal aspect.

It is, for instance, the only town I know that displays its former place of execution with quite such pride. If there is a guillotine twinkling in the sunlight for tourists to gawp at in Paris, I've never seen it. The Halifax model, upon which the one used in the French Revolution was based, is still there, on the way to the old ground at

Thrum Hall. It is one of the reasons Halifax was celebrated in song as a dreadful place; it was certainly a dreadful place to be caught stealing a bolt of cloth.

More of that a little further down the road. The town's more mundane miseries on the rugby league field have something to do with a fact we notice with some relief – it is far too close to Bradford and to Odsal in particular.

Strictly speaking, Bradford ends and Halifax begins a few hundred yards from Odsal, through Buttershaw but before the wonderfully named village of Shelf – you couldn't have airs and graces living in Shelf, could you? – and the natural dividing line for support for the two clubs should roughly coincide with the boundary. I'll bet, though, that the line has shifted a bit towards Halifax over the last couple of years and it may creep further yet. It is a while after the 'Welcome to Halifax' sign before we start to see much blue and white. There are compensations; away to our left, the landscape is opening up to show the most expansive views so far, over hills and woods towards Hipperholme – and the sun is shining. The Bradford and Great Britain doctor, Chris Brookes, is enjoying it and mounting a spirited defence of Keiron Cunningham. 'When somebody you believe to be qualified tells you that something is all right, you believe them. You wouldn't take it if you didn't.'

The spot chosen for the handover to our Halifax minders is called Stone Chair and waiting for us there are the requisite players, Lee Finnerty and Paul Davidson, and the man with the worst job in rugby league, Tony Anderson. Finnerty, who ended the year playing for Dinamo Moscow, is suspended – wrongly, he tells us in some detail on the way into the town. In one of the year's less predictable career moves, Finnerty supplied the match-winning pass when Dinamo became the first Russian side to win a Challenge Cup tie, beating West Bowling in December. Davidson – astonishingly, given his record – isn't suspended; he's injured. Their matching shaved heads make a couple of good mobile landmarks when we start bobbing and weaving through Halifax's shopping streets.

But the one I really feel for is Anderson. An Australian, but an adopted son of Halifax, he gave up a steady job as Shaun McRae's assistant at Hull to come back to a club he played for in far, far better days. The first thing he said of that decision, when I asked him about it the day he took the job, was that he already feared he had let his heart rule his head. People do that in rugby league. They give up secure, manageable jobs for insecure, impossible ones because they have a vision of the transformation they might be able to conjure. In Tony's case, part of the vision was of turning back the clock to recapture the spirit of the Halifax side he had played in – the heavily Australian-accented mid-'80s line-up financed by the local businessman, David Brook. I remember one match at Leeds when there were 23 Australians on the pitch; it was probably the day on which the idea of an overseas quota was first mooted, because things were getting out of hand. The Aussies at Halifax were a special bunch. Headed by stars like their player-coach, Chris Anderson (no relation), the wildly hirsute Geoff Robinson and the Test full-back, Graham Eadie, they were famous for working hard and playing harder. I can vouch for the truth of the latter part of the equation; a quiet social evening with them in the players' bar at Thrum Hall entailed about a week's recovery time. They had plenty of like-minded British teammates, like our mate from the scrapyard, Roy Dickinson, but the tone was set by the Aussies, who treated their time at Halifax like one long tour. Oh yes, when they briefly sobered up, they won the old First Division Championship and the Challenge Cup. Something strange happened the day they won the league. They needed one point to clinch the title; their opponents at Thrum Hall that day, Featherstone, needed one to avoid relegation. With the scores level at 13-all and what seemed like several minutes left to play, the two timekeepers, one from each club, agreed that was close enough and sounded the hooter. It was the sort of thing that might just spark a bit of discussion if it happened these days on live television – I can just imagine Stevo getting stuck into that one – but in those innocent times it passed almost without comment.

Tony tells a story which sums up those days. Another of the club's itinerant Aussies, Michael Hagan – now the highly respected and, no doubt, impeccably sober coach of the Newcastle Knights – was flying home at the end of his stint with the club, so naturally most of his fellow-countrymen wanted to see him off. 'It took us two days to get to Manchester Airport and two days to get back, stopping at every pub on the way.'

On the way back, the police started taking an interest in the packed vehicle's erratic progress. The driver was Bob Arnold, a big prop who knew he was several days beyond the limit, so, somewhere on the outskirts of Halifax, he screeched the car to a halt and everybody in it ran off in different directions, jumping over garden walls and into farmers' fields. Unfortunately, Arnold chose a wall that led, via a 20ft drop, into a river and injured himself so badly that he spent months in traction and hardly played again. Maybe it was sympathy, but he was never charged with anything. The story has an interesting postscript. A year later, a chap knocked on Chris Anderson's door and told him he had something for him. Wrapped carefully in a rag, he had a slightly rusted watch, with an inscription to Chris from his teammates at his Australian club, Canterbury. 'I was doing a bit of digging in the front garden and I found this.' Ah, happy days. With his watch back on his wrist, he went on to become Australia's Test coach.

The saving grace of the carousing mob that was Halifax was that when they got on the field to train or play, it was down to business. Tony Anderson goes all dewy-eyed at the memory of it and admits frankly that he would like to recreate the same ethos at the place almost 20 years later. The trouble, as I try to suggest gently to him, is that neither Halifax nor any other club these days is very well endowed with players of the playing ability of Chris Anderson, Eadie, Hagan and the rest, who also happen to have the social constitution of oxen. The reality was that the Halifax team of 2003 consisted of some, admittedly promising, kids who weren't quite ready, some lacklustre veterans and a sprinkling of overseas players who pretty much came and went as they pleased. Tony had had some harsh things to say about the level of commitment he detected in some of them and the upshot of it all was that Halifax were Super League's worst-ever club, with a grand total of no points. It would have been two, because – astonishingly – they had won their first match, at a well-fancied London Broncos. They had those points deducted, however, for a breach in their salary cap during the previous season – David Brook never had to worry about such niceties – although how a club with no money manages to overspend is one of those puzzles in which rugby league abounds. Although they never seriously threatened to win a game after that, Halifax did talk confidently about getting their finances in order, largely through the efforts of Stephen Pearson, a Liberal Democrat councillor who had recently lost his seat to the British National Party and who headed an 'advisory group' which was running the club's affairs – or trying to. He was the closest thing Halifax had to a chief executive, but, just after being taken to the match against Huddersfield which made relegation mathematically certain, he died of cancer at the age of 47. It was a black joke that said much about the club's state of mind at the time that someone remarked that there was no point in Halifax winning a game now, because they would be docked the two points for not having a chief exec. That is typical of some of the dark humour in rugby league. The same week, I heard about the funeral of a player at which one of his former teammates was asked why he wasn't one of the pall-bearers. 'I carried him for three years when I played with him,' he said. 'I'm not carrying him again now.'

This is the day of the Trek on which I truly feel we are fulfilling a social need. Tony Anderson has left training in the hands of his assistant and bunked off for what amounts to a session of therapy. If you had his job, you would probably find it a welcome dose of light relief to walk a few miles shaking a collection bucket. From Stone Chair, through Northowram to Stump Cross – you couldn't make up names like these – we swing into Halifax across Dean Clough, with its huge mill complex that is now an arts centre with fancy bars and cafés. Were we heading for Thrum Hall – and, even several years after its demise, I still find my trainers dragging me in that direction – we would be heading right, up Gibbet Street, with its grim monument, and out to the western fringes of the town that Priestley considered the hilliest in England. In his *English Journey*, he recalls that 'the trams, groaning desperately, go mountaineering'. When he was enlisted for the First World War, he was sent to the barracks on what he calls Gibbet Lane. I presume he means Gibbet Street, or maybe, like Wheldon Road, previously Lane, it has subtly changed its name over the years. It was a sunny September in 1914, 'but I can never recollect Gibbet Lane offering us anything but a Siberian bleakness', he writes. If it was Siberian bleakness he was after, he should have ventured a bit further uphill to Thrum Hall.

Mind you, the gibbet itself still casts a chill. Not that it would be much consolation if you were waiting to be dispatched by it, but it is a misnomer. It isn't a gibbet for hanging felons, it's a primitive device for beheading them, one which Dr Joseph Guillotine came from France to study. Its use is first mentioned in 1280 and, at that time, many towns in Yorkshire had a similar arrangement. What sets Halifax apart and accounts in part for the town's gory reputation is that it hung onto its robust regime of punishment long after it had been abolished elsewhere, a little like the Isle of Man with the birch, but a tad more final. As late as 1654, two miscreants named John Wilkinson and Anthony Mitchell were executed for stealing cloth. History doesn't record how much cloth they stole, although it would seem a little harsh for a pocket handkerchief. Still, as my dad would say, I'll bet they didn't do it again. They failed to take advantage of a Get Out of Jail card of sorts, local tradition decreeing that, if a condemned man somehow got out from beneath the falling blade and escaped across Hebble Brook, he could go free. It sounds like a good way of training resourceful and resilient wingers, although with a built-in rate of attrition. If you were convicted of stealing an animal – or doing something worse to one – the animal was tethered to the pin controlling the mechanism and was given the honour of triggering it, which could have led to some logistical problems if you were guilty of rustling a whole flock of sheep.

Up Gibbet Street, now an almost exclusively Asian area, is what remains of one of the most famous rugby league grounds in the world, one which, along with Oldham's Watersheddings, used to sum up the part that the Pennine weather used to play in winter rugby. With its slope and its feeling of complete exposure to the elements, Thrum Hall was a tough place to play the game. One Australian player, there for the World Club Challenge in 1997, was quoted as saying, in all seriousness, that he now had a feel for what the game had been like in 1895.

On the day I went back for a look, the sun was out and bulldozers were working on the supermarket that will eventually occupy much of the old site, which included a cricket ground and bowling greens as well as the rugby stadium. It is only the crown green bowling – another distinctively northern pastime – which has survived. That is now played on new greens on what must once have been the Thrum Hall pitch. The geography is difficult to fathom now; it is only the sight, down a back street full of washing, of a surviving stretch of wall, with a half-familiar blue door in it, that acts as a reminder of where things were. It reminds me, as well, of my favourite Thrum Hall story, concerning the time that Halifax ambitiously booked a team of sky-divers to drop in with the match ball before their first game in Super League. For some reason, they never turned up and a ball-boy had to be deputed to kick one over the stand from the back street in order to achieve the same effect. Several weeks later, one Monday afternoon as everyone was going about their business at the ground, there was a roaring of engines overhead and a series of six parachutists descended onto the pitch, one by one. They had got the day right, but not, unfortunately, the month. Like sky-diving, running a rugby league club is a precision business.

Back in the here and now, Halifax is a largely unreconstructed town in which the Halifax Building Society's modern glass headquarters looks oddly out of place. Tucked down a side street on the hill leading down to the station is one of the jewels of Yorkshire, one of the wonders of the West Riding. The Piece Hall – piece, as in pieces of cloth – is the only surviving manufacturers' hall in Britain. It's an open square surrounded by collonaded decks of little rooms, once used by 315 woollen merchants with their wares to sell – and heaven help you if you tried to pinch any. It's a glorious place, a little time-warp into which you can wander off the street. If it was in London or Florence, people would be queuing around the block.

Remarkably for such an unpretentious town, Halifax also has another unforgettable edifice which is amongst the most jaw-dropping of its type. Wainhouse's Tower, according to Headley and Meulencamp's *Follies, Grottoes and Garden Buildings*, is 'the best folly in the county, one of the finest in the whole country'. A folly, by the way, is defined by the *Shorter Oxford English Dictionary* as 'any costly structure considered to have shown folly in the builder'. John Edward Wainhouse originally built his as a chimney for his dye works, necessitated by the Smoke Abatement Act of 1870. He sold the dye works, but the new owner refused to continue with the expensive chimney project, so Wainhouse carried on purely for decorative effect – although his fellow industrialist and sworn enemy, Sir Harry Edwards, was convinced it was built to spy on him. From the ornate top of the slender, 275 ft shaft, you could spy on most of West Yorkshire, and playing rugby league in its shadow, as several Pennine League clubs do, makes you feel rather small when, ideally, you'd like to feel big and tough.

Talking of folly, however, we are on our way to The Shay. It is the historic home of Halifax Town, but the rugby league team flogged Thrum Hall and moved in with them in 1998. It was meant to be the financial salvation of two impoverished clubs, but it didn't quite work out like that. For one thing, the money from Thrum Hall was agonisingly slow in coming through. Town, despite Russell keeping their feet in the best of order, were a club in decline as well, and they had no money either. They remind me of the two tramps in *Waiting for Godot*, bickering endlessly about their situation and hoping that someone or something is going to turn up and sort it all out.

The Shay – or is it still optimistically called The New Shay? – was supposed to be rebuilt as a dual-use stadium for the two sports. To an extent, it has happened. It has two new standing ends, something we probably thought we would never see built again in this day and age, and a serviceable stand down one side, where I always seem to be sat in front of a man who, despite his white stick and ceaselessly barking guide-dog, appears to be able to spot an opposition offside from 80 yards away. As you approach The Shay, though, you can soon see that something is wrong; the other side, five years on, is still a building site, all exposed girders and half-finished brickwork. There is no building going on; in fact, the last I heard, there was a risk that some of the steelwork might have to be dismantled, putting the whole process into reverse.

One thing already reversed is the club's unloved nickname of the Blue Sox. At a time when other clubs were becoming the Rhinos and the Bulls – bringing down a tidal wave of mockery on the game – Halifax thought they had better do something as well. The trouble was that they couldn't decide what to call themselves. I rather liked the Halifax Halibut, but it didn't meet with universal approval. In the end, the then chief executive, Nigel Wood – now the finance director of the Rugby League – decided that, instead of risking controversy by selecting a name that some people liked and some didn't, they'd go for one that everyone hated. Hence the Blue Sox. It's one way of achieving a consensus.

It was, of course, doomed. It became one of those names, like the Hull Sharks or the Oldham Bears, that was destined to be jettisoned because it was too raw a reminder of a stupid time in the history of a club. With it went, praise be, the mascots, Billy and Bluey. Other clubs might have an endearing animal character, like Ronnie or Bullman, or, at a less exalted but perhaps more imaginative level, Dewsbury's Roger the Ram. After ten pints and a quantity of hallucinogenic drugs you might just warm to one of these merry figures, but Halifax's equivalents seemed to be based on brattish children with quite severe learning difficulties and were every bit as irritating as any of those clowns who make real children cry inconsolably at circuses. Their costumes now feed the moths and the world is a happier place for that, although I note with alarm that they made a brief comeback at the end of the season, when they were pictured doing something or other in one of the trade papers.

Headley and Meulencamp do not list the unfinished stand at The Shay among their inventory of the nation's follies in their seminal tome, but in its own way it has every right to be there. In a way that typifies rugby league, however, people make the best of it. There is still the shell of a building under the steelwork and, in one of its rooms, volunteers are busily frying bacon and sausages to sell in aid of the Trek to those who turn up to see us pass through. These are the people who will make sure that, however grim times get, there will continue to be a rugby league club in Halifax, maybe not one that will ever win trophies again like it last did in the '80s, but still something for local kids to aspire to as they brave the icy winds blowing around Wainhouse's Tower.

The Shay is slightly off-route, necessitating a little back-tracking towards the town centre. First, however, there is another diversion to be made, for a photo-shoot in the car park of the local Tesco. The supermarket chain had been supporting the Trek by keeping us fed and watered whilst on the road. Every day, the support crew would go to the local branch, present their credentials and stock up with enough victuals for us and anyone else who came along. Naturally enough, they tended to give us the perishable items, like sandwiches, that they were having trouble shifting from the store by normal means, so I can vouch for the waning popularity in West Yorkshire of egg and cress, as well as tuna and sweetcorn. For some reason, we were required to drink copious quantities of Diet Coke for the cameras and that had not really been the beverage of choice at any stage of the trip. But needs must.

Doubling back, we go under the railway line and up the hill towards Siddal. This is a famous name in amateur rugby league – one of the strongest clubs in the country at the time of writing – and their ground is in a spectacular setting high above the valley. I was last here under unusual circumstances almost four years earlier, watching Siddal beating the Northside Saints from Dublin in the first round of the Challenge Cup, something that would have been difficult to imagine a few years before that. OK, Siddal put 90 points on a side many of whose members seemed to have been all too handsomely entertained at Dewsbury Irish Club the previous evening, but what the hell. Not far away, but at a slightly less elevated level, both topographically and in playing terms, is a club with one of the most resonant names in the game – or certainly in Division Two of the Pennine League – Greetland All Rounders. Not for them the narrow specialisation that restricts the game elsewhere. All these lads can play in any position, turn their hands to any other sport, write one-act plays, get stones out of horses' hooves and fix your gutters, or that's what their name has always seemed to me to aspire towards.

Climbing on through the village of Exley, we are already in the company of Paul Dixon, another of the Good Guys of the game who we knew would respond to the invitation sent out to all former Great Britain players. Paul is a hill-farmer and, although we already seem quite high up, he describes the location of his farm as 'up there somewhere', pointing up into the skies. He played his rugby like a man used to working hard for his living, playing above his always modest weight for Huddersfield, Leeds and, most of all, for Halifax. He also played 15 times for his country, his attitude to that honour being encapsulated by a conversation I once heard him having with a teammate. This other fellow was saying that he didn't think he'd be going on the Great Britain tour for which he had been selected, because his wife wasn't keen on the idea of him being away for ten weeks – this was still in the era when we had something resembling proper tours, albeit nothing like as long as the old six-month trips Down Under. 'What about your missus?' he asked Dixon. 'Is she letting you go?'

'Letting me go?' said Dicko quietly and without rancour. 'She dun't have a right lot of say in it.' More Pennine hill-farmers with straightforward, unreconstructed attitudes like that and I don't think we would have waited 33 years (and counting) to win the Ashes.

We drop down into the town of Elland, above which the Fairbank family – with dad and five sons, all of whom played for the local amateur club before graduating into professional rugby league – run their farm. The best of them, the Bradford forward, Karl, had to fix up for someone to do the milking before he could go on tour.

Climbing steeply out of Elland, with those of us with two breakfasts and a surfeit of Diet Coke inside us feeling the strain and Stevo complaining more pathetically than at any stage so far, but still managing to stay at the front of the group, we go through the aptly named hamlet of Elland Upper Edge, cutting across on an idyllic country lane to cross the footbridge over the M62, whilst the support vehicles take the long way round. Since 1971, vehicles have been roaring underneath – now to the tune of around 90,000 a day, most of them at exactly the time you tend to be crossing the Pennines for a night match – completely changing for all time what must once have been a lonely spot on the back roads to Huddersfield. It's a good excuse to stop for a while and stand and stare. Naturally, the conversation has turned, from time to time, to the desperate state of the club at Halifax, for which Dixon had played with distinction in such incomparably better times. One matter we were all agreed on was that his old teammate, Tony Anderson, despite his little holiday with us earlier in the day, had bitten off more than he could chew, that he had indeed let his heart rule his head. That was the sort of folly that a hard-headed realist, with mud on his wellies and a stretch of windswept moor to farm, would never dream of falling into. So, naturally, a few weeks later, after Tony had kept what was almost a deathbed promise to Stephen Pearson by agreeing to stay on as coach, Paul took the job of football manager at the de-Blue Soxed Halifax RLFC – the one role that would seem to guarantee more grief and frustration than merely coaching them. It's a big rebuilding job there, on the field as well as off it, with most of their better players inevitably leaving and some obvious difficulties in putting a competitive side on the field for 2004. One thing, though: I bet he didn't have to ask anybody's permission when he took it on.

VII

Huddersfield: Deviating Somewhat

IT'S A SHAME FOR MIKE STEPHENSON THAT OUR ROUTE FAILS to take us through Dewsbury, although by the time we get to Huddersfield we will have just about surrounded it. Had they been allowed into Super League when they won what was then the Northern Ford Premiership in 2000, it would have been a different matter. We would have had to go through Dewsbury, whether we liked it or not, with all the killing of fatted calves that would have entailed. But Dewsbury, like Hunslet before them, were turned away at the gates of heaven, thus saving us several miles, although I doubt whether that was the rationale at the time.

Stevo is something close to royalty in Dewsbury, as I found years earlier when I went there with him to call on his mum and dad. His mum, as all good parents should, has bequeathed him a store of good anecdotes, as in the time she rushed onto the field when he was a schoolboy learning the dark arts of hooking. She had spotted from a distance that, in those days, it was by far the daftest, most dangerous position on the field. 'You come out of there right now, Michael,' she shouted down into the front row, 'and make someone else have a turn.' She worries now that he won't be able to manage with just a part-time job, because he's only on Sky for a couple of hours a week. He was captain when Dewsbury won the Championship in 1973 and the big wad of money they got for him when Penrith's representatives came over from Australia and interrupted him in the middle of a plumbing job in Harrogate kept the club going for years after that.

The area around Dewsbury and Batley is one of those places, like the Copper Belt in Zambia or the Ivory Coast, named in perpetuity after its main product, even if it doesn't produce very much of it any more. This is the Heavy Woollen District, where its amateur clubs play for the Heavy Woollen Cup, and it is not at the glamorous end of the trade. The most conspicuous building you see as you come into the town centre advertises itself as 'Manufacturers of Mungo and Shoddy', which are, apparently, fabrics made from old rags and cloth in what sounds like an act of textile cannibalism. I couldn't promise to recognise mungo or shoddy – and certainly not to distinguish one from the other – if I was swathed in several itchy yards of the stuff and I'll bet you couldn't either, but I do know that it's not used for diaphanous scarves and fine-knit twin-sets. However, you could probably knit a decent hooker out of mungo and shoddy – if you had a pair of needles big enough.

Even though we don't walk through, Stevo and several others get to a fund-raising dinner thrown for him in a pub on the edge of town. He returns chuckling over one of the comedian's jokes, which he proceeds to tell to everyone who comes newly within earshot over the next week. I think it's a good joke, but not that good. You judge for yourself.

A chap from Dewsbury goes on holiday to Malaysia, where one of the attractions at the hotel is a beautifully manicured golf course. On his first day, he is practising hitting a few balls when a small crowd of locals gathers around. He strikes the first one sweetly enough, but he is amazed by the enthusiasm of their reaction, as they run around in circles shouting 'Tiger . . . Woods . . . Tiger . . . Woods!' This is all right, he thinks, teeing up another and smacking it into the far distance. This time they go absolutely berserk, screaming 'Tiger . . . Woods . . . Tiger . . . Woods!'

And then a tiger comes out of the woods. It gets better after the 28th telling.

* * *

Deprived of the cultural pleasures of Dewsbury, we walk parallel to the M62 as far as the roundabout at Ainley Top, with a hotel which, under its various names, has been privy to more than its share of rugby league intrigue in recent years. It's a very convenient location for clandestine meetings, arm-twisting sessions and the hatching of plots. We turn left down the straight and dull main road into Huddersfield. This is one instance when I really would have gone a different way, down Grimescar Lane – not just because of its name, but because it leads to Fartown.

Although they left it ten years ago, Fartown still lives on for Huddersfield supporters in more ways than one. Even at the McAlpine Stadium, you can still hear shouts of 'C'mon Fartown', making them surely the only team to remain popularly known by the name of their former ground. At least they don't make the mistake of an old girlfriend of mine – who, I'm beginning to think might have had a milder case of Ken's problem with words – who always used to refer to them as the Fart Owners. You don't hear people at the JJB Stadium shouting 'C'mon Central Park'. OK, Fartown is also the name of a part of the town, but I doubt whether we'll hear Warrington fans, relocated to the other side of their town centre, chanting 'Play up, Wilderspool'.

So Fartown has proved an unusually memorable ground and what's more it still survives in a recognisable form. Needless to say, there was no time for a sentimental side-trip in Uncle Bernard's relentless schedule, so we went back a couple of weeks later to see what was left of it. You can still go through the main gates, where there used to be a sign proclaiming that this was 'Arena '84, the home of the Huddersfield Barracudas' – the first, doomed attempt by a club to revamp its image. If any younger fans think they had the piss taken out of them unduly when their club adopted a risible nickname at the start of the Super League era, they should have been Huddersfield supporters in 1984, because they were in the stocks of public mockery, being pelted with rotten eggs and tomatoes, all on their own.

You can still pass the memorial to the great Yorkshire cricketers, George Hirst, Wilfred Rhodes and Schofield Haigh, before crossing the pitch on which they played. It was Haigh who, weighing up the

 1. Stevo gets some early encouragement at the KC Stadium, Hull
(courtsey of Philip Wilson)

 2. Nick Barmby and Shaun McRae at the start
(courtsey of Philip Wilson)

 3. The starting point – the banks of the Humber
(courtesy of Ken Cross)

4. First day line-up, featuring Johnny Whiteley (centre, not drinking) and Scott Walker, pushed by Graham, the Drinks Man (courtsey of Philip Wilson)

5. Merging in with the locals in Castleford (courtsey of Ken Cross)

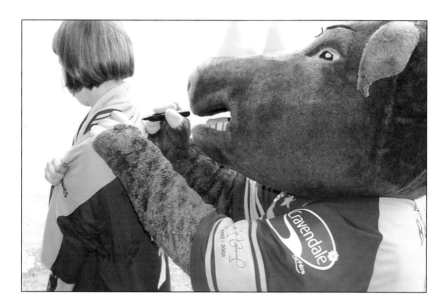

6. Ronnie signs in (courtsey of Philip Wilson)

7. Outside the hotel where Eddie Waring didn't live, with Barrie McDermott and Kevin Sinfield (courtsey of Philip Wilson)

8. Volunteers waiting in the rain at the Leeds–Bradford frontier (courtesy of Ken Cross)

9. Proper hills, proper views (courtsey of Philip Wilson)

10. Retail therapy for Tony Anderson in Halifax (courtsey of Philip Wilson)

11. The author at Siddal: 'How much further? I can't look' (courtsey of Philip Wilson)

<table>
<tr><td>12.</td><td>12. In Huddersfield – the birthplace of rugby league (courtsey of Philip Wilson)</td></tr>
<tr><td>13.</td><td>13. Brian McDermott leads the way into Saddleworth (courtesy of Ken Cross)</td></tr>
</table>

14. JJB Stadium – home to the Wigan Warriors
(courtsey of Philip Wilson)

15. Crossing the M62 for the last time
(courtsey of Ken Cross)

| 16. | 16. With Ray French in Warrington – why, oh why did he have that bet on the momentum rule? (courtesy of Ken Cross) |

| 17. | 17. Warrington's new stadium takes shape (courtesy of Ken Cross) |

18.

19.

20.

18. Ready to beat the drum for the last leg of the Trek (courtesy of Ken Cross)

19. Widnes' car park never looked as good (courtesy of Ken Cross)

20. Signed and sealed – the campervan at the end of the Trek (courtesy of Ken Cross)

possibilities of an inviting seamer's wicket in these parts, uttered the immortal assessment: 'Methinks they'll deviate somewhat.' You just can't get quotes like that these days, methinks, not from cricketers, rugby players or prime ministers.

It's when you get to the old pavilion, familiar to generations making their way to the rugby turnstiles, that things start to turn odd. It is now the Pavilion Party Ranch, advertising its availability for weddings, christenings and the like. A semi-derelict cricket pavilion might seem an unpromising place to tie the knot, but the lady hanging her washing on the line behind it says it does pretty well. She also directs us up the cricket terracing – they used to get big crowds for that as well – towards the remains of Fartown. It still has a perfectly good pitch, used by Huddersfield for their Academy games, and the once massive North Terrace, which looked out on Harold Wagstaff and the Team of All the Talents, which dominated the game before and after the First World War and is perhaps still the greatest of all club sides, is still there, although not looking so massive these days, now that its upper reaches have gone back to nature. The whole thing is surrounded by new railings, but there is the plaintive sight of one remaining antique turnstile and two equally ancient dug-outs. There is also the supporters' club, from which I can remember Alex Murphy surveying training on rainy nights in the early '90s. Through the windows, I can see that they still have their magnificent collection of framed cartoons of great Huddersfield players, all resplendent in one of rugby league's finest colour schemes, claret and gold. Our friend with the washday duties says they still get a decent turn-out to the club. So there's your answer: Huddersfield supporters have never quite left Fartown, spiritually or physically, although I see that since my visit the club has stopped using the ground.

The other good thing about this road is that it leads you into Huddersfield past the Slubbers Arms, a wedge-shaped pub that is a particular magnet before and after games. To slubber, by the way, is described in my grandad's old dictionary, which is the only sort of dictionary in which you can expect to find it, as 'to do lazily, imperfectly or carelessly; to stain; to daub'. It's the staining and daubing that's relevant here, I suppose, and it sounds like the sort of thing you might do to any mungo or shoddy brought over the hill from Dewsbury. 'I'm just slubbering the shoddy,' they might have said in those days. I don't think any advertising agencies had a big say in naming the products or the processes.

Despite those connotations – and the time that I saw one of Huddersfield's French players robbed in the street outside – the Slubbers is a salubrious establishment; far more so than a pub nearby into which I once wandered, in all innocence, before a game at the McAlpine. Taking the top off a pint, I happened to glance up at a TV screen above the bar and, blow me, there was a couple going at it like knives, as they say in these parts. Looking around nervously, I saw that there were several screens, all of them showing the same intimate exchanges, some of them watched by semi-interested drinkers, but most of them completely ignored by those sitting or standing right in front of the TV, who were more interested in eating their crisps. I knew that this was not ideal preparation and could easily take the cutting edge off my match report, so I looked for a side-room where I could escape these scenes of debauchery. In I went and there was the couple off the telly, live and in the flesh, giving it their best shot on the pool table, with a cameraman straining for the best angles and a few blokes sipping pints of lager and occasionally glancing over to see how it was going. I don't know what Harold Wagstaff would have made of it. There didn't seem to be much guilty subterfuge about it either, because I noticed, as I went out, large signs reading 'Live Sex Show', which I had somehow overlooked on the way in. And this in a country where you will soon need to jump through all manner of bureaucratic hoops and fork out for a licence before you can have two people strumming a guitar and singing 'Dirty Old Town' in your pub. Who knows where that sort of thing could lead?

* * *

Our actual route into Huddersfield is routine in the extreme by comparison, but it does have the advantage of leading into a square which, in rugby league terms, is as full of history as Trafalgar, Tiananmen or St Mark's, if rather less full of tourists. There is something equally monumental, almost in an Eastern European way, about Huddersfield's equivalent, with its impressive railway station running across the top of the square and the statue of Harold Wilson, caught in mid-stride walking away from it, as though he's just arrived on the 10.48 from Westminster. The Labour prime minister represented what was then a rugby league constituency – Huyton – but he was very much a Huddersfield man, with the result that, to those of us of the right age, an educated Huddersfield accent still seems to imply a pipe firmly clamped between the teeth. Wilson was a football devotee, which made him the follower of an upstart code. In the West Riding, as Robert W. Lewis remarks in an article called 'The Genesis of Professional Football' for the *International Journal of the History of Sport*, football was a latecomer, often via clubs like Halifax, Huddersfield and Leeds City, planted and fast-tracked in rugby areas to try to give the round-ball game a truly national spread. You have to acknowledge that they succeeded, which makes it a bit of a laugh when people insist that it is impossible for rugby league or any other sport to grow on alien soil. Historically, that couldn't be further from the truth.

We come into the square – which, if rugby league ever needed to stage a mass rally, would be the only possible place – down a cobbled street that leads into one of its corners. Diagonally opposite is a building without which, and without what happened there on 29 August 1895, none of us would have been there – the George Hotel.

The George is the holy of holies as far as rugby league is concerned, the birthplace of the game, thanks largely to its proximity to the station for the Lancashire delegates to the meeting which sent rugby league off on its own track. Historians, who have made a more detailed study of the events leading up to that day than I, have argued to and fro about its significance. Michael Latham and Tom Mather, in *The Rugby League Myth*, contend persuasively that there was never any intention of breaking away from the Rugby Football Union, over the issue of broken-time payments or anything else, and that the leading northern clubs merely wanted to reorganise their fixture lists. It was certainly not a meeting of working-class heroes, breaking out from under the heel of the southern gentry, however satisfying that version might be. Geoffrey

Moorhouse, in his acclaimed essay, 'At the George', says that the men who met there 'were not much different in substance from the men who led the conformist rugby clubs further south'. One example he quotes is Tony Fattorini, who represented Manningham – a highly successful early Northern Union club that eventually switched codes to become Bradford City – and who was a maker of medals and trophies. Fattorini's made the original Challenge Cup and must have expanded their repertoire in subsequent years, because we bought our wedding rings from them – partly because of the rugby league connection – and also have one of their ornate clocks, no longer operational, in our hall. Fired by a similar sense of history, we obviously have to go inside for a drink.

Turn right from the main foyer and you get to the room in which the fateful meeting is supposed to have taken place. There is an understated little plaque on the wall to that effect and some framed shirts. If that seems a little low-key, you should have been here a few years ago, when there was nothing at all to acknowledge the hotel's role in the genesis of the game.

It's a laborious business getting a drink, with the bow-tied young barman pulling each pint – and we want a few – as though it is his first, but it gives us time to reflect on our surroundings. The George is now a tiny part of a bigger hotel empire, but in recent years the game has started to reclaim it. There is a good historical display in another of the main reception rooms. In 1995, the game's centenary celebrations were launched here, but just as quickly sank, because its administration at the time hadn't got a clue what it was supposed to be celebrating. It was also here that, on 11 September 2001, a group of us were meeting to select British rugby league's all-time best XIII when we were told that we had better turn the television on. A second plane was just flying into the World Trade Center and the question of whether Whiteley, Turner or Karalius was the greatest loose-forward was never resolved. More recently, a body called 1895 International has taken to organising events here. At one, a couple of months after we passed through, several hundred people spent the day watching a triple-header of the National Rugby League Grand final from Sydney and the National Leagues One and Two Grand finals from Widnes on the big screen. The waiters wore T-shirts bearing the legend: 'Rugby League – Chess with Muscles', and the money raised went to support a tournament in the Lebanon. The 1895 International even has its own permanent office at the hotel and BARLA's Maurice Oldroyd wants the game's Hall of Fame to go there as well. The reclamation of the old shrine goes on apace and so it should, because, whether that was the intention or not, this was the scene of a revolution.

The word often used to describe it is schism, which has the right degree of religious undertow to place the events that led to rugby league in their true context in the English dissident tradition, which produced Methodism in 1795 – a neat 100-year gap – and Harold Wilson's Labour Party. The legacy has not been entirely positive, because the game has been prone to schism ever since; it was in Huddersfield that the British Amateur Rugby League Association set up shop when it decided to take control of its affairs and, if you wanted to see schism within schism, then a close watch on that organisation over the years would have been instructive, because, just like Nonconformism and progressive politics, it has had the inbuilt tendency to splinter and fragment. I once went to Fiji and although there were only a handful of clubs and players, there were two mutually antagonistic governing bodies.

For all that, I've never, even in my darkest hours, had any doubt that we were on the right side: honesty versus hypocrisy; democracy versus autocracy; labour versus capital; La Resistance versus Vichy; matches decided by tries rather than goals. Whatever confused impulses made us move that way, we were on the side of progress, rather than reaction. It is a theme I tried to explore in a publication which disappeared into the void that opened up around the game's centenary in 1995. It is the only thing I have ever written about rugby league for which I would go cheerfully to the gibbet; I hope you will forgive me the self-indulgence of quoting from it now, because I don't think anybody read it at the time.

> There are two sorts of history. There is the history of kings
> and queens and empires, of church and state and
> establishment. And there is the history of dissent and

subversion, of people who stand up and say 'No, that's not the way it's going to be'.

As we look for our place in the sun and wrestle for our slice of the corporate cake, we need to remember that we are part of that latter tradition. We are not quite respectable; there is a hint of the outlaw and the renegade about us. And that, as we start our second century, is not a weakness. If we will but realise it, it is our most enduring source of strength.

Bloody hell, I used to go on a bit in those days.

* * *

If the George is full of echoes of the past, the future of the game in Huddersfield is represented by the McAlpine Stadium, a mile down the road on the way back to Leeds. I'm there that weekend for their home game against Hull and there's no mistaking the fact that the club is on the rise once more. It has taken a while. For years, the Huddersfield Giants were a running joke in Super League and were finally relegated when they finished rock-bottom once too often. Worse than that, in many ways, was the fiasco of their merger with the Sheffield Eagles. Post-Hetherington, the Eagles – always too far away from the M62 for some tastes – were losing money hand over fist, but had some decent players. Huddersfield had a benefactor with deep pockets, but a dismal team. Put them together and what do you get? Well, probably an unloved hybrid with Sheffield's finances and Huddersfield's inability to win a match. It was a nonsense. It wasn't quite rugby league's stupidest moment of the 1990s. I refer you for that to the later chapter on Cumbria – oh yes, we're going that far – but it wasn't far off. Huddersfield and Sheffield have nothing in common with each other apart from being in Yorkshire. They couldn't even decide what the merged club should be called. There was a push for the Giant Eagles. The estimable John Ledger at the *Yorkshire Post* always referred to them as Shuddersfield, not to be confused with Bruddersford, the fictional Yorkshire town – with a rugby league club – in which J.B. Priestley set many of his stories. In the end, they settled for the Huddersfield-Sheffield Giants and that was what they remained until quietly dropping the Sheffield bit, for it to be picked up by Mark Aston, who restored them to an independent status.

Meanwhile, Huddersfield finally went down, but kept a full-time squad together and, under the coaching of Tony Smith, bounced straight back. In 2003, they were still widely expected to fall in a heap again, but they proved tremendously difficult to beat at home, where their scalps included, that mid-Trek Sunday, Hull. There was just one cloud on the horizon. Their chief executive, Ralph Rimmer, confided that he was resigned to losing Smith, although he wasn't sure to whom. There seemed to be two possibilities. Wigan were in the market for a coach at the end of the season, Stuart Raper having decided to go home to Australia, a decision made easier when the club did not offer him a new contract. The informed word, however, was that Smith had been lined up as the inaugural Super League coach of Union Treiziste Catalane, the Perpignan-based side who were supposed to restore the French link – severed when Paris St Germain were shown la porte – to the competition. The truth about his destination, when it emerged a couple of days later, was stranger than either of those alternatives.

On this particular match-day, though, the main mood was one of euphoria at once more being the sort of team that could win games at the top level. People were shouting: 'Well played, Fartown.' Tim Adams, the man responsible for dragging Sheffield Eagles up the M1 and allowing them to be swallowed up by the Giants, no doubt with much fee-fi-fo-fumming, was so ecstatic that he shoved a £20 note for the Trek into my top pocket. Just to show that there were no hard feelings, I left it there.

* * *

The route resumes outside the George, on a day when our numbers are swollen by an unprecedented number of day trippers, ready to tackle what was simultaneously the most challenging and the most rewarding day's walking of the two weeks. There was the League's Andrew Whitelam and the statistician Ian Proctor, who was no doubt well aware that we were due to walk 19.3 miles with a height gain of 758 feet, into a headwind blowing at 14.75 kilometres per hour – the strongest in Huddersfield on a Sunday since October

2001. Even more significantly, there was my mate Keith, who was taking my dirty washing home for me, and Brian McDermott – no relation to Barrie, but, confusingly, sometimes his rival for a place in the Great Britain front-row. Brian was due to be at the McAlpine for his duties as the Giants' fitness coach later that day, so his timetable was a tight one. He got around that by transporting everything he was going to need – boots, tracksuit, a few dumb-bells – in a rucksack. You would say that amounted to carrying too heavy a handicap, but Brian is not only a recently retired workaholic rugby league forward with the Bradford Bulls; he is also a former Royal Marine and professional boxer. I'd call that a pretty good array of credentials for climbing a few little hills.

As soon as you cross Huddersfield's ring-road, the climb starts, alongside the River Colne and the Huddersfield Narrow Canal. As it becomes gradually more rural, we go through the village of Linthwaite. If there is anywhere on the route where I might be tempted into an ill-judged diversion, this is it, because just off the route is the Sair Inn, home of the Linfit Brewery – which is how they say Linthwaite round here. There are usually eight or so of their beers on the bar and, one day on the way home from a Huddersfield game, Keith and I sampled them all – and he couldn't have many because he was driving. There are always a few old hippies and wolfhounds steaming in front of the open fires and the menu runs to the underrated culinary experience that is the pickled egg. Nothing else – just pickled eggs. Paradise . . . but it is an hour and a half before opening time and a 45-degree climb up the hillside, so the moment passes. Next up is Slaithwaite, although I bet that's not how they pronounce it. Something closer to Slowit, I'm told by my local spies. Talking of dialect, by the way, we are shortly to leave the area where quite young people might still be caught using the word 'laik' where the rest of us would say play. Through much of Yorkshire, a good player might equally well be a good laiker, although I don't think that is why the Los Angeles Lakers are so called. It comes from Old Norse, my *Dialect Atlas of England* tells me, and survives in areas settled by the Norwegians and Danes. They say 'laik' in the Sair.

A little further and a little higher is Marsden, maybe my favourite small town in Yorkshire. They brew their own beer here too – and celebrate Cuckoo Day. It also marks the start of the Standedge Tunnel – the longest ever built for a British canal at 5,698 yards (Ian Proctor made a note of that) and recently reopened. I've been trying to persuade Andrew Whitelam for a couple of years now that it would be the ideal place to launch the Origin Game between Lancashire and Yorkshire, because you go into the tunnel in one county and come out of it, three miles later, in the other. You could send the two captains through on a barge for a photo opportunity and, if you wanted to be strictly traditional, make them power it themselves by legging their way along the walls of the tunnel. That sounds as good a training regime as stoking the boilers on HMS *Indomitable* on the way to Australia in 1946 – and we know what happened on that tour (drawn one, won two). Andrew says he'll get back to me, but since then the League has abandoned ship as far as the Origin concept is concerned.

* * *

As we rise up past Marsden, with the entrances to the canal and railway tunnels away to our right and the old pit-workings up the slopes to our left, we are at our closest to another Pennine landmark. There can be few people so dead of soul as to have travelled the M62 without wondering about what life must be like at the farm in the middle of the motorway. If you've been that way once, you will have noticed it; if not, it is between the Ripponden and Huddersfield turn-offs that the carriageways suddenly split and create an island a mile long and about a hundred yards wide at its maximum, with a white-painted farmhouse stranded in the middle of it. This is Stott Hall Farm and it is a famous symbol of Yorkshire stubbornness. The story goes like this: a gritty tyke put up the barricades, defied the government and the road-builders and refused to move out of the homestead that lay directly in the line of the road, forcing them to spend extra millions in going around him. It's a good story, with the authentic whiff of Yorkshire bloody-mindedness about it, but it's also absolute rubbish.

What really happened is that the road planners always intended to split the road at this point, because there isn't enough solid ground on either side of the farm to hold all of it. Rather than have the disruption of moving, the farmer was happy enough to stay, although folklore has confused him with one of his neighbours, a little further from the motorway but a lot angrier about it, who used to take pot-shots at the bulldozers' wheels with his air-rifle, so presumably wasn't quite as reconciled to it. In a recent documentary on Radio 4, the man at Stott Hall came close to admitting that, had he known there would one day be up to 100,000 vehicles tearing past, he might have thought again, but otherwise he seemed pretty philosophical about it. They have had to put up with various cargoes – including sheep, schoolbooks and fine bone-china – spilling onto their land, as well as the odd accident victim, and they have taken it all in their stride. His wife, though, sounded a little plaintive when she recalled the time the motorway was closed for a week by a landslide and, for the first time since 1971, she could be out in the farmyard and hear the bacon sizzle in the kitchen. They aren't heroic in the sense that millions of passers-by have always assumed, but that doesn't spoil the story for me. Like so many things around here, the truth – that of people choosing to live like that and being quite content with it – is more compelling than the fiction.

Like the legend of Eddie Waring in the attic and the story of the serfs revolting at the George, the Siege of Stott Hall Farm is pure myth. But we need our myths and this is one we should build upon. I know Steve Ball is looking at various sites along the M62 for his statue embodying the spirit of rugby league, but I'd like to propose the farm at the fork in the road. I'm not entirely sure what putting it there would say about our particular brand of Northern Englishness, but it would say it in a sufficiently ambiguous way to be thought-provoking.

* * *

Up on the A62 the big moorland scenery is starting to unfold, with Saddleworth Moor, with its doleful reputation and still undiscovered graves, to the south and the marginally gentler country of Marsden Moor, studded with reservoirs, to the north. It's hard to imagine this now as one of the main routes over the Pennines in the pre-motorway days, but it was this way that teams and supporters used to travel to matches and its isolated pubs were famous meeting places for trans-Pennine transfer deals, much as Birch Services is now – except that, the last time I went past, someone had burnt the westbound services to the ground. That's the sort of thing that could have disrupted the economy of the entire game, had the transfer system still been its driving motor in the way it once was. As it starts to rain, some of us dive into one of those lonely pubs, but it is one that the landlord and landlady seem intent on keeping lonely. They have a system which I don't think I've seen before, whereby they like you to pay for your beer before they pull it, presumably to guard against you taking a quick gulp and doing a runner. This is taking the natural mid-Pennine suspicion of strangers to new heights. What do they think you're going to do? Dash out and lose yourself in the crowds? They weren't keen on us eating our Tesco sandwiches – egg and cress or tuna and sweetcorn – in their best room either.

Back on the road, Brian McDermott – bless him – confides that he's finding it hard going. The walking, that is, not Stevo's jokes. That'll do me, I think; if it's all right for a boxing ex-Marine fitness guru to be getting tired – albeit one with a multi-gym on his back – it's OK for me too. In any case, we have a sure-fire spirit-lifting moment coming up as we approach the Lancashire boundary – Greater Manchester, technically speaking, but you can imagine how much house-room we give to that concept. Ken has materialised from somewhere amid the bog and bracken, mysteriously rejoining us, so it must be an important stage in the journey. Behind us, that strange, murky place they call Yorkshire, none of it any clearer to me for a week's immersion in its odd ways as we walked across it; ahead, the sunlit – and it's amazing how often the weather changes completely, for better or worse, as you cross the watershed – hills and dales of God's county.

VIII

The Land That Super League Forgot

I HAVE A MORAL DILEMMA OVER SADDLEWORTH. AS A BORING stickler for the old, proper county boundaries – if I'd been born 100 miles further south-east, I would have been a militant Rutland nationalist – I should be prepared to admit that it really belongs to Yorkshire. But the fact is that it's too good for them and certainly too good to give up without a fight. I'd be prepared to cede other areas far bigger and more populous – they could have everything east of Blackburn, for me – but Saddleworth is too precious to lose.

It's a well-kept secret. Everyone knows about Saddleworth Moor and the unmarked graves, but down in the valley is a hidden little world of its own. It has everything you could want. Tiny Saddleworth League cricket grounds perched on hilltops or squeezed into valleys. Inter-village brass band contests, the biggest of them held every Whit Friday. A dozen of the best pubs to be found anywhere in the country. A string of delightful, delicious, delectable backwaters: Diggle, Dobcross, Delph, Denshaw – and that's just one letter of the alphabet. And rugby league, of course. From the point where we turn off the main road, opposite the sadly defunct Floating Light, we can see it all spread out in front of us like the Promised Land.

Until 1974 and Ted Heath's Local Government (Reorganisation) Act, this was part of Yorkshire, but, if you walk here from

Huddersfield, it undeniably feels west of the Pennines, as though it should be downhill all the way to Piccadilly. Diggle, where the rail and canal tunnels emerge blinking into the sunlight, is the first of the D-villages. Surely a tunnel from Yorkshire to Lancashire is more convincing than one from Yorkshire to Yorkshire. Sounds conclusive to me; we're in Lancashire – or, rather, Greater Manchester – although some recalcitrant factions, still loyal to the old regime, stubbornly celebrate an annual Yorkshire Day. The tunnels are a reminder that Saddleworth was once far more familiar to the outside world than it is now. Travel from Manchester to Leeds by barge, train or car and you went through it. Now the M62 passes it by, the trains still go through but don't stop and, although the Huddersfield Narrow Canal is open again, not many travel that way for anything other than a stress-relieving holiday. We stride down the main drag; another case of going the wrong way, because there are spectacular hilltop routes on either side of the valley. There are compensations on the lower ground, however, like the classic Saddleworth scene of a square in Uppermill being prepared for brass band activity. Half an hour later and coincidence could have given us what would have seemed like a full ceremonial welcome to Saddleworth. This is a cultural hotspot in another sense. Dialect poets, the rap artistes of their day, were massive here. As well as the obelisk that acts as a monument to Saddleworth's war dead, there is a less conspicuous memorial up on the tops to Ammon Wrigley, who not only carried that tradition into the twentieth century, but was also a distant relative of the family that emigrated from Saddleworth to set up the chewing-gum dynasty in America.

A little further on, occupying one of the few stretches of flat land, is Saddleworth Rangers' ground. They are struggling a little at the moment, but, for several years, they were arguably the best amateur side in the country. It is possible to climb on a steep footpath from Greenfield Station and look down onto the pitch far below on the valley floor. It is, I would submit, the best view of a rugby league ground anywhere in the world – the one that the gods would choose if they were keen followers of the First Division of the National Conference, but didn't want to pay the £2 to get in. I can tell you from bitter experience that it looks a lot better from up there at a safe distance than it does from close quarters, with the hail driving into your face from the direction of Diggle and Dobcross and Rangers' second team putting 50 or 60 points past you. Up on the top of the hill behind the ground are the odd and rather precarious rock formations called the Pots and Pans. One day, hopefully not during a match, some sudden lurch of the earth's crust is going to send one or two of them rolling down into the valley. It's just a matter of time.

Swinging right after Uppermill, we skirt Greenfield, Grasscroft and Grotton; we're onto the G's now, don't ask me what happened to E and F. It soon becomes apparent that there is something wrong with my mental map of these parts. Far from it being a nice stroll downhill into Oldham, it involves another steep climb. So that's the secret of Saddleworth's geographical ambiguity and the mystery of its identity; it's up the hill and over the top from both sides of the Pennines. Further down Oldham Road they are cramming some fancy new commuter houses into a place called County End. This is where Yorkshire started and finished before Ted's men got to work on the map – deep in the suburbs of the unequivocally Lancashire town of Oldham. If Oldham can have suburbs, that is – a point on which I'm far from convinced.

* * *

For a competition which lives, breathes and has its being along the line we are tracing across the north of England, it is an awfully long way between Super League clubs once you leave Huddersfield. Personally, I'd support a Saddleworth franchise – the Delph Donkeys, perhaps, in memory of the trains on the now closed branch line, which were so called – but I suspect they are behind Perpignan and Bridgend in the queue. More to the point is the impact the revolution in the game over the last decade has had on the string of towns and cities which come next.

There is a tremendous amount of bilge talked about whether things are better or worse since the coming of Super League and summer rugby. To listen to some of the True Believers, the game was not merely dying in 1995, it was stone dead. They came along and reinvented it and everything has been onwards and upwards ever since. In the traditionalist corner, there are those who honestly believe that everything in the garden was lovely and that the events of the mid-'90s ruined the game they loved. Neither of these sets of beliefs stands up to much scrutiny, but the one with which you have the more sympathy will depend largely on where you are looking at the game from. Among followers of the elite clubs and even those on the fringes who have adapted to the changes, without quite being able to elbow their way onto the top table, the majority view would be that their circumstances have improved. Gates are up; the presentation is slicker; television money finances full-time professionalism, so the spectacle is faster and, it is easy to argue when the top teams play each other, the standard of play is higher.

For those outside the charmed circle, the reality is very different. Life for rugby league clubs outside the top division has never been easy, but it has become a good deal more difficult and unrewarding. For instance, take Oldham. (Purlease . . . as the inexplicably popular local comedy duo, Cannon and Ball, might once have said.) Despite Oldham Athletic's brief but breezy foray into the Premiership, it definitely feels like a rugby town. If we had a Town of Origin competition, it would be able to call upon the old Headingley car-pool of Barrie McDermott, Iestyn Harris and Kevin Sinfield – an Oldham-born player who won Leeds' Player of the Year vote four years running – plus the Sculthorpes. It would also have a good claim on the services of players like Tommy Martyn, Chris Joynt and Paul Deacon, who began their professional careers here, just as Andy Goodway did in his day. There was even an Oldham equivalent of Stella Street, where, in one of the posher parts of town, Mike Ford – now drawing a handsome salary for his part-time job teaching Irish rugby union players how to tackle, which is not a turn he ever imagined his career taking – lived next door to Paul Sculthorpe, with someone who looked very much like Michael Caine across the road. If Huddersfield is the birthplace, then Oldham can claim to be the first home of rugby league, because it was here that it set up its original headquarters, if only because its first honorary secretary, Joe Platt, was an Oldham man.

For all that, Oldham have traditionally found success difficult to achieve and impossible to sustain. That is why the *Oldham Evening*

Chronicle's Roger Halstead is one of the people in rugby league journalism I admire most. In his long stint reporting on the club, he has seen them go up and down the divisions more often than he can count, almost get to Wembley on several occasions and implode on several others. By the time he hangs up his quill, he will have been diligently chronicling this endless cycle of false hope and disappointment for uncomfortably close to 50 years; and the tragedy of it is that, if everyone had their own, he's really a Rochdale Hornets supporter.

Had we taken a slightly earlier exit out of Saddleworth, it would have been possible to descend via Grains Bar past Watersheddings, a ground which, until it had houses built all over it, had a grimness of aspect and an absence of creature comforts which made a visit to Thrum Hall seem like watching a match from a tart's boudoir by comparison. Never has a ground been more aptly named, because I can never remember a dry day at Watersheddings. Its altitude could also have another effect on occasion. I remember going there to watch a New Zealand tour game on a day when it was cracking the flags in Bolton, people were sunbathing in Bury and still in their shirt-sleeves in Rochdale, but Watersheddings was frozen solid. The Oldham Tinkers came close to catching the atmosphere of the ground in one of their ditties:

> At Watersheddings it used t'be good
> To see them fight for t'ball in t'mud
> But now the game has changed, dust see.
> You can't have fighting on TV.
> Eddie Waring is a bum,
> Eddie Waring is a bum,
> Ee-I-Addi, Eddie Waring is a bum.

Before the old place was sold and pulled down – just before it fell down – it did see Super League, when the Oldham Bears finished as high as eighth in the first season of the new competition. Ah, the Bears . . . another name that can never be spoken in its home town without people spitting on the floor. They are the Roughyeds now again, of course, which meant the demise of the game's most lovable mascot. It was a local amateur player called Braddy who donned the rather moth-eaten bear costume and it was quite clear from watching his inspired antics that he knew the game. He proved that in irresistible style during one match against Warrington, one of whose inebriated supporters came onto the pitch and cleaned him out with a blatant off-the-ball tackle. As the perpetrator stood taking the acclaim of the Warrington fans behind the sticks, Braddy dusted himself off, ran in from 20 yards and very nearly cut him in half with a shoulder into the small of the back. Not only has the recipient not tackled a mascot since, he is only just tackling solid food again. Braddy has since gone on to bigger things, as the original Ronnie the Rhino, before a big-money transfer to Bradford, where he became Bullboy. He once stopped me in my tracks at Burnley by whipping off his head and revealing that he was also the man in their bee suit, but he has never quite recaptured the magic of the moment when he gave that coaching manual demonstration of how to tackle from behind whilst dressed as a bear.

Oldham dropped out of Super League and, not for the first time in their history, collapsed in on themselves. They have since been involved in one of those carping Samuel Beckett relationships with the Latics, have spent various spells in exile at Rochdale and Ashton, and will not, barring a miracle, be back in the top flight in the foreseeable future. If Super League has made a difference to them in their current situation, it is that the gap between where they are and where they still aspire to be is that much harder to bridge.

There's nothing to see at Watersheddings now, so it's not much of a tragedy to be walking into town along the other route, through Lees and Salem – whose club, Salem Hornets, had one of the better names around these parts. Before Mumps – with its bridge bearing the proud boast 'Oldham – Home of the Tubular Bandage' that used to be a landmark on the way to and from the 'Sheddings – is a way of cutting through to the ground of the town's most successful amateur side these days – Oldham St Anne's. Peter Deakin was something close to a ghostly presence alongside us for much of this walk. He was a major influence at Warrington as well as at Bradford – who noted on the day that they won the 2003 Grand Final that it would have been his 50th birthday – but he was an Oldham man. He learnt his rugby at St Anne's and it was to their clubhouse that we repaired after his funeral earlier in the year. Being there was as uplifting as it could have been under the sad circumstances, because so much of what had been achieved at that little club was down to him and his family. He had always claimed – with his mania for every helpful scrap of publicity – that the goalposts he had procured for St Anne's were the tallest in the amateur game. I took advantage of his wake to go out and have a look at them and I have to demur. I reckon the ones at Eccles – which used to be at Station Road – are higher, but that is one argument we will never have.

Oldham has a nasty 1960s shopping centre, designed primarily as a wind-tunnel and particularly bleak on a Sunday afternoon, with no bodies to shelter behind. It is at this point that we lose fellow travellers, like Brian, Andy, Ian and Keith, who have more pressing things to do the following week. For us, the following morning means the long, straight road to Manchester. As we go along there are two sights worth noting and one piece of news to digest. The first sight is the Oldham Rugby League Supporters' Club, newly opened in an attempt to give the game a focus in the town. It's another sign that they don't really feel at home at Boundary Park. The nearest licensed establishment is the suspiciously named Smut Inn. I can't help wondering what their idea of entertainment is there, and whether it bears any relation to that on offer at that pub in Huddersfield, about which I told you so reluctantly.

The news concerned the Wigan coach, Stuart Raper – appropriately, a former Oldham player, who told some good stories about being snowed into the house the club's Australians shared and having to climb out through the window. The rumble out of the JJB for some time had been that he was losing the dressing-room, something that was perhaps best illustrated by a well-publicised outbreak of impromptu wrestling outside a Wigan pub after a day out with the squad. The moment you really knew he was on borrowed time, however, was when the club's owner, Dave Whelan, went onto the field during the warm-up before one home match and delivered the pep-talk to the players. From that time, Raper was fatally damaged goods and, sure enough, after a home defeat by

Widnes, the announcement came that he was being relieved of his duties with immediate effect, with no particular instructions as to whether he should leave by the door or the window. It made it an interesting time to be heading for Wigan.

Failsworth has something I never knew it had – a monument marking the site of its old maypole. It's not the sort of thing that would normally stop me in my tracks, but, after 120 miles or so, it's surprising the things you can find interesting. On we press towards the big city, which should, in some ways, be one of the focal points of the whole trip. Manchester is, after all, the undisputed sporting capital of the north of England and the centre of its media and communications. It just happens to have a bit of a blind spot where rugby league is concerned. It is almost half a century since it lost its own club – Belle Vue (formerly Broughton) Rangers – and although the code has traditionally played some of its biggest fixtures in the city, at Maine Road and more recently at Old Trafford, it feels as much like a visitor to Manchester as it does to London. Salford, a vast conurbation in its own right but visible to the outside world only as the rough end of Manchester, is a different matter, but rugby league occupies little of the attention in the middle of the big city. They found this out on one Kangaroo tour. Perhaps a little wary of how enthusiastically the players were fêted when they stayed in Leeds, the management decided in their wisdom one year to base them in Manchester instead, on the grounds that they would be mithered less. For a few days, being left pretty much alone was a welcome novelty to players who had been here before. By the end of the trip, though, they had realised the disadvantages of being just an anonymous bunch of big blokes in green tracksuits. In Manchester, there was nothing like the regular supply of food and drink, red-carpet treatment at casinos and enthusiastic young ladies that they had grown used to in Leeds. By the last week, they were walking around desperate for someone to mither them. It was an experiment that was not repeated.

It hasn't always been the case, but Manchester is now a depressingly solid bastion of football orthodoxy, as though, by the time it has finished dwelling on the fortunes of United and City, it has little time left for anything else. United even took over

Broughton Rangers' picturesque ground at The Cliff as their training base, until they moved to the 'Gulag' at Carrington. City fans might be able to write books entitled *Manchester United Ruined My Life*, but only Broughton Rangers' supporters can claim that they nicked their pitch; that is the way the balance of power has swung. Rugby league fights for a little corner in the *Manchester Evening News*, amid the page after page devoted to burning questions of the day, like whether Paul Scholes or Nicolas Anelka take milk in their coffee. Rugby league is something for the outlying districts, not for the city itself. Small wonder that the arrival of a few weary-looking blokes walking from Hull to Widnes failed to spark off huge demonstrations of support or any ticker-tape welcome. You don't need any expensive marketing campaign to assess where rugby league means something in this country; all you need is Mr Michael Stephenson, who can be used as an accurate barometer of public opinion – a Stevometer, even – to gauge the level of interest. In unassuming little towns like Knottingley and Normanton, he was greeted like a conquering hero; in Manchester, the general assumption was that he was selling the *Big Issue* and people crossed onto the other side of the street. Maybe it was just time for them to go back to the office, but I got the distinct impression that by parking up in front of the Town Hall and having our lunch – cheese and mayonnaise and BLT seemed to have been moving slowly in Greater Manchester's Tesco stores that day – we cleared Albert Square more effectively than a bomb scare. It was definitely time to head back to Rugby League Land and start getting mithered again.

Fortunately, that doesn't involve going very far. The city of Salford lives cheek by jowl with Manchester, albeit in a deeply unequal relationship, and, as soon as you cross the Irwell, you're in it. There is a shiny new Salford now, the place of Salford Quays, of blocks of flats revamped for yuppy living, of the Lowry – named for a man who was specifically a Salford, rather than a Manchester artist, but who, unfortunately, tended to paint crowds going to football matches, rather than rugby. They have even cleared up the Manchester Ship Canal, a stretch of water once so polluted that anyone unfortunate enough to fall in was immediately taken to

Salford Royal to have his stomach pumped. Now they pump oxygen into the canal and there are fish, Canada geese and even the occasional cormorant to symbolise the revitalisation of the derelict docks. But we are going through unreconstructed Salford, which is a byword for urban decay and roughness. That means going down Liverpool Street, the name of which reveals that, however run-down it might be now, it was once, before the East Lancashire Road and the M62 were built, the road that linked the two great cities of Lancashire. This is the industrial Salford in which Friedrich Engels formulated his theories. It was the original Dirty Old Town – a song I was once delighted to hear sung by a gang of Salford fans on the train on their way back from Widnes, segued with a paean of praise to their then hero, Bobbie Goulding, set to the tune of 'Bob the Builder'. The oral tradition lives on. A mucky old metropolis it might still be, but you get a warmer welcome in the string of Joseph Holt's pubs – notable for selling the cheapest beer in Britain to some of the thirstiest customers in Britain – along Liverpool Street than you would in the glossy bars of mid-Manchester. When we're ushered into one, full of the sort of characters who are expecting to spend all day and most of the night in there, it's free pints from the landlady and hands in pockets from all the drinkers. They get Sky in that pub, so they know exactly who Stevo is and what he's doing. Some nine- or ten-year-old scallies out on the street aren't quite as sure.

'Where you walking to, mister?'

'Widnes.'

'Fuckin' 'ell.'

Welcome to Salford. It has a bit of an image problem, especially around the Langworthy Road area, which has been used in numerous printed and broadcast horror stories to illustrate just how low urban decline can go. As ever, it's an over-generalisation; amid the tell-tale signs that the crack-heads have taken over parts of it, there are the equally unmistakable signals of ordinary people doing their best. I can't get sniffy about it; there are too many gardens better tended than mine – even if they sometimes have a richer crop of syringes – and too many house-fronts better painted. A little further on, one block back from Liverpool Street, is Cedric Street, where Adrian Morley grew up. Mozza couldn't join us on the Trek, on the rather flimsy pretext that he was in Australia, bishing and bashing his way towards a second successive Grand Final, but he volunteered to give me a quick tour of his mean streets when he got back to Britain a few weeks later. To read his Australian press cuttings, you would be totally convinced that he had grown up in one of the less salubrious parts of Beirut, in a place where the paper boys carry guns. Well, some of them might, but the Aussies – as is their wont – rather overdo the heaven–hell dichotomy. OK, he now lives near the beach in Coogee in Sydney's Eastern Suburbs, which is pretty close to paradise, but his upbringing in Salford wasn't quite as hellish as they like to make out.

'They like to make it pretty black and white,' he says. 'They've sometimes phoned my old mates back home about what it was like growing up here, but they only use the juicy bits.'

One theme on which these Redemption of Mozza stories tend to dwell is the absolute certainty – quotably reinforced on occasion by the man himself – that he would have embarked on a life of crime, had it not been for rugby league. Not if his folks had any say in it, he wouldn't, because they are rock-solid, respectable working class, not the wasters that central casting would like the entire population of Salford to be. His mum was the lollipop lady on the crossing we are walking past, as well as a dinner lady at the school across the road – and you don't get any more pillar-of-the-community than that. His dad never missed a day's work and made him go to church until he was 16, after which he was free to make up his own mind. As rough goes, it wasn't. 'Now, down there,' says Mozza, pointing towards Eccles New Road. 'That was rough. I used to be too scared to go down there.'

Now that he's the most intimidating forward in world rugby league, with Aussie skulls hanging from his belt, we think we might just risk it, over there on the wrong side of the Metrolink tram tracks. A lad whips past on a chopper bike, hood pulled down to largely obscure his face. They exchange wary acknowledgements.

'Hiya, Mozza.'

'Hiya, Smiffy . . .'

'Now he,' says Mozza, as he pedals off about his dubious business, 'is one of the bad lads round here.' Didn't mess with us, though, did he? We are somewhere between Weaste and Seedley here – I've never been quite sure where the dividing line comes – with The Willows up Weaste Lane to our right. It was here that a young Adrian Morley honed his skills by standing in the street outside to catch any balls kicked out of the ground and – this being Salford – run home with them to add to his collection. If Salford have their way, they won't be kicking balls into these backstreets for much longer, as they have plans for a state-of-the-art new stadium on the other side of the motorway at Barton. The club has become convinced that the location of its ground is one of its major obstacles when it comes to attracting a wider public. It wasn't always like that. In the late '60s, when Salford had their own version of the Team of All the Talents, spearheaded by major rugby union signings like David Watkins and Keith Fielding, The Willows on a Friday night was the place to be and the sports and showbiz glitterati of Manchester used to be there – Bobby Charlton, no less. There was a novelty then in having a variety club attached to the ground and, for a while, it seemed that Salford might be leading the way forward. All the big names played The Willows, although I remember some friends going to see the Four Tops and coming away sceptical about whether it had been the original line-up, because three of them were white.

It might be a little harder to attract United and City players to The Willows now. The sight of what was once Weaste Cricket Club, overgrown to head height behind the cantilever stand, is a reminder of the problems. They stopped playing and abandoned the ground a couple of years ago, after their clubhouse had been burnt down once too often. The rugby club has great difficulty trying to keep its ground secure as well. If they do ever move to Barton, it's only vandals with cars they'll have to worry about – that and whether they can stay in Super League, promotion back to which they were in the process of winning as we walked past in July.

Seedley (or is it Weaste?) is the area of Salford in which *Coronation Street* is set. If Weatherfield has a local team it is definitely Salford RLFC, or Salford City Reds, as they now like to be known. Occasionally, a character with rugby league connections will appear – most recently, the dodgy builder, Dougie Ferguson, who seemed to be solidly based on one or two ex-Salford players, and who came to a sticky end when a banister, not so solidly based, gave way in one of his shonky flat conversions whilst he was arguing the toss with the sinister Richard Hillman.

Up Weaste Lane, we go past Mozza's old school – a call I made with him on our later visit – where he was turned on to playing rugby league by an enthusiastic teacher. He is the original Mount Carmel boy made good, but his old headmaster agrees with his own assessment that he was 'quite good academically, but a bit of a lad'. One change is that the school is now called All Hallows; another is that it is now surrounded by high railings. 'To keep out you lot who live round here,' says the head, looking meaningfully at his distinguished former pupil.

Over Eccles Old Road, it turns quite posh, before reverting to something more recognisably Salfordian at that tongue-twisting destination, Irlams o'th'Height. There aren't many from the wrong side of the Irwell who can pronounce that correctly. It is here that I fall prey to temptation. There is a number 8 bus to Bolton going past every ten minutes and it's ten days since I've seen my granddaughters. I've become slightly obsessed with being a good grandad because that's something I think I can manage. I want to see my children as well, of course, but that is a pleasure weighted down by responsibility and being a good father is one of those impossible jobs, like managing Leeds United, coaching Swinton or leading the Conservative Party. However hard you try, you're going to get it hopelessly wrong.

Back home, I display those tell-tale signs of having been on tour, or, in this case, involved in a near-tour experience, like leaving sweaty kit lying around for the maid to clear up and calling room service at three in the morning. It might be better if I come back and start again when I've got this out of my system.

* * *

Resuming the following morning – scrupulously from the same spot, for anyone thinking of claiming a refund on their sponsorship money – we find ourselves in the company of Dean and Mike, manager and coach of the British Prison Service team. Not only is this, and the Civil Service generally, another of the game's growth areas, they can also claim to be the only side since Lord knows when to go to Australia and come back unbeaten. Naturally, the subject of the Headingley Two crops up. They are the latest in quite a star-studded line-up to pass through the hands of Dean, Mike and their colleagues. 'Don't worry,' they say of Messrs Walker and Bailey. 'We'll send them back fit.' Cheaper than La Manga, as well.

We're soon in Swinton territory, or what *was* Swinton territory when they were a force in the game. We go past the cottage where a promising schoolboy rugby league player named Ryan Wilson – the son of Swinton's maverick genius, Danny – spent his formative years. He changed his name to Giggs and disappeared completely; I often wonder what happened to him. A little further on is The White Lion, the pub that was Swinton's early home and which gave them their nickname – one which has proved a little more durable than the Sharks, Bears or Blue Sox. In a back room is the Swinton Hall of Fame, a reminder that, in their heyday, the Lions had some of the finest players in the game – including, from their early '60s side, Ken Gowers and Alan Buckley, who used to run the pub across the road. The room doubles up as the pub's long-established folk club and there is a poster on the wall advertising a weekend at Salford University devoted to the work of Ewan MacColl (born Jimmie Miller, in Salford), who wrote 'Dirty Old Town', 'The First Time Ever I Saw Your Face' and about a million other songs, both topical and timeless. He was the offspring of Scots who came to Salford for work; Swinton, in the club's first great era, thrived on the labour of Welshmen, come north because they could combine playing for pay with the day jobs the club had in its gift. The Lions' early ground was across the road and the stadium at Station Road, which was once one of the most important in the game, a little further up on the right. There is nothing there to see now, apart from that particularly soulless housing that always seems to take over historic rugby league sites – I have a theory that it brings bad luck, like building on a Red Indian graveyard – nothing apart from the old supporters' club on the corner, now used by the amateurs of Folly Lane. As for Swinton, they have become another of the lost, nomadic tribes of rugby league, spending ten years in the wilderness in the stubbornly uninterested town of Bury, before coming back a little closer to home. If they have a future, it is as a local club with limited horizons, but there is nowhere for them to play that is truly local to their roots.

Veering off to the left, we are soon in leafy Salford, in the wealthy suburb of Worsley, where the Bridgwater Canal is bright orange from the minerals leached out of the surrounding soil and where Great Britain go into camp before Test matches. The manager of that team, Phil Clarke, is getting jumpy. We are closing in on Leigh and, as a highly identifiable Wiganer, he always smells a bit of hostility in the air there; Stevo reckons he gets the same thing in Batley. As we go through Boothstown and across the East Lancashire Road – the M62 of its day, but mystifyingly named, because the one place it doesn't lead to from any direction is east Lancashire – Phil's getting broody and by the time we get to Astley, he's looking ghastly. A mate of mine used to live in Boothstown – so did Eric Cantona, but that's another story – and he told me how often he was woken up by vehicles rushing out from the Mines Rescue station there. Pit disasters were a fact of life around here, where the seams are deeper below the surface and more dangerous than in Yorkshire. There was usually some rugby league connection; I remember one player who put his back out carrying a coffin after the Golborne Disaster and was never the same again.

The other thing that runs deep in Leigh is resentment of the big brother that Wigan is perceived to be. The two were bundled together under Local Government Reorganisation, but being bracketed in with 'Bigwiggin' has always rankled and, when the local casualty department closed, you can imagine the outcry. Add to that the way that the local rugby league team – a match for Wigan, thanks to players like Des Drummond and John Woods, through the '70s and early '80s – plunged into decline just as Wigan were becoming the most successful club in the world and you have the makings of a first-class chip on both shoulders. I still think Phil is overdoing it when he puts a Tesco bag over his head at the 'Welcome to Leigh' sign, but a little later I see that he might have a point. We are all wearing Outward Bound T-shirts with a succinct but inspiring message on the back: I Can. As I'm spending most of the Trek looking at people's backs, I've found it helpful. Most people along the way have given us an occasional 'Course you can', to keep up our flagging spirits. Leigh is the first place where people slow down, lean out of their car windows and shout: 'I bet you bloody can't!'

Leigh is another of the places that produces a disproportionate number of rugby league players and we soon pass one of the reasons. It was at Leigh Rangers that players like Denis Betts – despite being a Salford lad – cut their teeth. It's now part of Leigh Miners-Rangers but remains one of the best conveyor belts in the game. The team that used to play out of The Eagle and Hawk, a little further up the road, was less a conveyor belt than a dumping ground. I played for them in a series of matches against local sides in London on the Sunday mornings after Cup finals and the pattern was always the same. Northern know-how would give us a healthy lead and southern hangovers would guarantee us a sickly second-half collapse, which we would survive by a shrinking margin every year. After scraping home by a disputed drop goal, we decided to call it a day.

If there is a patron saint of the drop goal, it should be Alex Murphy. There should be a statue of him somewhere near the point where we cross the main drag, because no club's fortunes have been tied to one man's comings and goings the way Leigh's have to his. A few weeks after the Trek, he was reappointed at Hilton Park – just down the road to our right – for a record-shattering fifth time. I was there for his fourth coming, when there were cameras in the changing-room, waiting to capture his shock reappearance and carefully scripted first line: 'I expect some of you are surprised to see me.'

It took a while. The first time the door flew open, it was with the words: 'I'm surprised some of you expected to see me.'

'Cut!'

'I see some of you expected to surprise me.'

'Cut!'

Eventually he got it right: 'I expect some of you are surprised to see me.'

'We might be,' muttered one old head. 'If it wasn't the fourteenth time you'd come in.'

Another classic Murph story – there are a million – concerns the time he came to see the Leigh directors with his phone bill, on the grounds that most of it was run up wheeling and dealing in the transfer market on their behalf. After some discussion, they agreed to take care of it. The following week, he came in with his electricity bill, to be told that they didn't see why they should pay that as well. 'You mean you want me to make phone calls in the dark?' he asked.

Up Twist Lane, just before Leigh Miners' ground, a group of ladies have turned out in their dinner hour to greet us – and to prove to Phil that not all Leigh people are bitter and twisted. We cross Atherleigh Way, which runs along the route of the old Bolton–Leigh railway line, which has claims to being the first in the world to carry passengers. As much as anywhere, Leigh was the epicentre of the transport revolution, but cuts and closures left it with four pubs called The Railway, but no station. As we go up Wigan Road, I'm as close as I get on this trip to my tenuous roots in rugby league. Steve, my best mate at school, lived just around the corner and The Tamar is where we did a good deal of our underage drinking. He was one of a little tribe of lads from this neck of the woods – him, Trevor and Dave from Leigh, Mel, John and Johnny from Atherton, Cliff from the wilds of Daisy Hill. Almost without exception, they were good sportsmen and were soon roped into school football teams, which hardly interested them at all, because what they wanted to do was play rugby league. There was no chance of them being able to do that officially, not at a grammar school in Bolton in the 1960s. Instead, they organised league matches among themselves, with a few big, dopey specimens like me to make up the numbers, whilst, for the school, we played a heavily league-accented version of rugby union. That's how I come to be retracing my steps through Westleigh almost 40 years later and writing this book.

When we were about 15, Steve and I went to the offices of the *Rugby Leaguer*, which was then the game's only publication and was based in St Helens, to try to get signed up to write a few articles. His mum went ballistic. To her, getting involved professionally in rugby league – even if it was only ten bob for writing a few paragraphs – was one step from going down the pit, as his dad had done and she was determined that he never would. That wasn't what she had sent him to grammar school in Bolton for, not by a very long chalk.

Steve used to live on Nel Pan Lane, which should give a clue to the fact that they have their own language around here. Granada once made a documentary about a group of Westleigh lads, going about their business, playing a bit of rugby, going fishing; despite it only being shown in the north-west, it still needed subtitles. The dialogue and its translation went something like this:

'Wilt goo t'Leyth morn?'

(Would you care to accompany me on a visit to Leigh tomorrow?)

'Morn morn or morn neet?'

(Are you proposing this expedition for tomorrow morning or tomorrow afternoon?)

When it was announced a few years ago that the Royal Yacht *Britannia* was to be moored in Leith, near Edinburgh, I bet there were people on Nel Pan Lane who thought it was going to be tied up on the spur of the Leeds–Liverpool Canal alongside Leigh Miners' ground. There is a good deal of thee'ing and thou'ing around here, too; as in 'Don't thee thee me, thee' (If you address me as thee, you must face the consequences) which is fighting talk in these parts.

Back in The Tamar, Andy Wilson of *The Guardian* has introduced a very worthwhile practice, celebrating his short walk with us by not just contributing to the fund, but also buying the participants a pint. With him, the Wigan youth guru, Brian Foley, and the England Students' coach, Lee Addison, all in tow, we press on past one of the more vividly named takeaways of the trip – 'The Leigh-ning Tower of Pizza'. Nowhere in Leigh, however, could I see lobby advertised. Lobby is one of the ways in which Leythers like to express their distinctness from Wigan. It's basically meat and potato pie without the crust, but the absence of crust is absolutely crucial, as much as the exclusion of various meats from the more diet-sensitive of the world's religions. They can be called lobby-gobblers without it being as insulting as it sounds like it should be. But, as we emerge in Hindley Green, there is a defining moment. My friend Dave – another Dave, not mentioned yet, whose twin passions in life are Wigan rugby and bluegrass music – lives just across the road. I get a cheery wave from his wife, Lynn, who is queuing up for a late lunch at the corner shop. It is a pie-shop and the queue stretches out of the door. The signs are unmistakable; we have crossed the great divide and we are, to all intents and purposes, in Wigan.

IX

Wigan: Tripe, Pies and Rumours

WIGAN HAS WHAT MY OLD GRANNY, WITH HER DISTINCTIVE
way with words, would have called an ambidextrous relationship
with the man who did more than anyone – more even than Maurice
Lindsay – to put it on the map. On the one hand, it is quite happy
to clutch him to the bosom of the local branch of the heritage
industry; Wigan is as much George Orwell Country as Haworth is
Brontë Country. On the other, the town has always been
uncomfortable with what he said about it, or what it thinks he said
about it. Whenever some new Orwell link is inaugurated, there is
always a dissenting voice asking why Wigan should celebrate
someone who slagged it off so comprehensively. There was even the
woman, maybe some distant relation to my granny and possibly
apocryphal, who said: 'I could never stand him. Him or his stupid
little ukulele.'

That woman, if she ever existed, was closer to the truth than she
knew. It was George Formby Snr – the father of the man with the
stupid little ukulele – who incorporated the idea of Wigan Pier into
his music hall act and the use of the term to denote an illusory or, at
best, profoundly disappointing destination was already embedded
in the language before Orwell purloined it for his *Road to Wigan
Pier*. For a book which has done so much to set the town's image in
aspic, it is astonishingly non-specific. Orwell split his two months'

research between Wigan, Barnsley and Sheffield and he flits between scenes from the three places, often with no indication of exactly where we are. The well-known visual images of the down-trodden unemployed and squalid living conditions in the Penguin edition have nothing to do with Wigan; they are photographs taken in South Wales, the Northeast, Scotland and even London. All the same, when Orwell is at his most vivid, describing the working conditions in the mines and the filthy state of the lodging houses in which he stays, it is often clear that he is talking about Wigan. That was the problem for a lot of readers in the town; they didn't mind being told they were poor and oppressed – a lot of northerners take a perverse pride in that – but they didn't like being told that they were mucky. One thing is certain: you will never fancy tripe again – if you fancied it in the first place – after reading his description of what it was like behind the scenes at a Wigan tripe-shop.

Orwell never mentions rugby league, although it is a fair bet that in 1936 many of the people he met would have been pretty interested in the game. Wigan had won the Championship in 1934; in 1936, maybe even whilst he was in town, 14,000 watched them beat St Helens, who were not even particularly good opposition at the time. That notorious tripe-shop was on Darlington Street, a few minutes from Central Park and even closer to the pitch where Wigan St Patricks now play. His other lodgings, on Warrington Road, are now on the way to the JJB Stadium, but he could hardly be blamed for not knowing that. The closest he comes to acknowledging the game is in his description of the importance of pit-head baths, which were a recent innovation at some of the bigger collieries. He says of this lucky breed of cleaner miner that 'within twenty minutes of emerging as black as a Negro he can be riding off to a football match dressed up to the nines'. I like to think that the match in question would be rugby league football, but it is not a subject that interests Orwell. As a public-school educated, upper-class southerner – for all his socialist sympathies – he was looking at the people of Wigan as he might have done an exotic foreign tribe and he decided what was important.

Wigan now pays its homage to him in a variety of ways. The pub at Wigan Pier is called The Orwell. A more subtle and meaningful tribute, however, is that the inevitable town centre Wetherspoon's takes its name from an imaginary pub he described in his column in the *Evening Standard* in 1946.

'My favourite public house, the Moon Under Water, is only two minutes from a bus stop, but it is on a side street, and drunks and rowdies never seem to find their way there, even on Saturday nights.'

It is a nice touch using Orwell's pub name, even if the real pub has little in common with his invented ideal, because this is a town that has not always taken much care with its drinking heritage. The best pub in town, The Park, where you could sit beneath framed action pictures of Wigan games – the landlady was the widow of a former director – and press a bell to have your Walker's mild and bitter brought to you, was demolished, not just for a nasty new shopping centre, not even for the attached car park, but for the bloody ramp leading to the car park! In a final act of irony, parts of it salvaged from the ruins are now on display at the heritage-fest that is Wigan Pier. That and the stubby little stump of what was once a jetty from which coal was tipped into waiting barges. Orwell couldn't find it in 1936, but he could hardly miss it now, not with signposts leading to it all the way from the motorway.

* * *

On our way through Hindley Green and Hindley into Ince, Phil expounds on the pie business. Wiganers, as everyone is surely aware, are known as pie-eaters. In my naivety, I had always assumed that this was simply because they eat a lot of pies, which they most assuredly do – mainly meat and potato, or, if the ingredients are listed in quantity order, potato and meat, or potato, potato, potato and a rumour of meat. I know vegetarians who eat them with a clear conscience, but only a true Wiganer will tackle that triple-carbohydrate treat – a pie barm (bun, bap, flourcake). (See Chapter II.)

The facts according to the Clarke household are quite different. Phil claims that, during the General Strike of 1926, Wigan's miners were the first to be forced back to work and a local newspaper carried the headline: 'Wigan Miners Eat Humble Pie'. So, calling them pie-eaters is rather more of a slight than the simple dietary observation it might appear to be. But Wigan is proud of its pies. The only memorable mascot its rugby team has had since stumbling into the Super League era was a pie on legs and nothing Dave Whelan has done during his stewardship of everything that matters in the town has brought down the opprobrium on his head that shutting Poole's pie-shops did. That left the way open for independent operators like one corner shop we passed, which bore the proud sign: 'Winner: *Wigan Observer* Pie of the Year Competition'. Who needs the Oscars when you've got something like that going on?

Naturally, on a diet like that, Wiganers are the strongest people on earth and one of our calls on our way through Ince is at Royce's Gym, which specialises in wrestling as well as in all the standard instruments of torture. Many of the great Wigan players of the past – Brian McTigue and Roy Evans are good examples – were accomplished wrestlers; not grunt-and-groan or WWF, but proper Olympic wrestling – boring to watch, but demanding great strength and coordination. The other refreshing thing about Wigan is that everybody knows everything about rugby league, whether they've been to a match for the last 20 years or not. A Wiganer who has never seen a game or a newborn Wigan baby, in fact, knows more about it than a non-Wiganer who has spent his life studying every nuance. Everybody in Wigan already knows everything about the game that appears in the paper before it appears, except that they also know the parts that weren't used – and why. It must be something in the water, or more likely in the pies.

We have already passed Hindley RLFC, a relatively new amateur side that has nonetheless produced a healthy crop of professionals, and up ahead, near where a couple of lads are wrestling with pies, is the most famous nursery of them all, Wigan St Patricks. If they were to list all the players from this club who have made a living in the game, they would need to tag on an extra storey to accommodate the honours board, but you can start with Andy Gregory and work downwards, taking in the likes of Phil Clarke on the way. St Pat's are one of the reasons why the town of Wigan supplies players to clubs all over the north. I remember Blackpool Borough reluctantly deciding not to sign another, because the 12-seater minibus that came over from Wigan on training nights was full. Eventually, they bowed to the inevitable and started training in Wigan instead.

If the timings are right, you can watch a match here in the afternoon, wander down the towpath of the Leeds–Liverpool Canal – another trusty reference point on this trip – for a pint in The Orwell and on to the JJB Stadium for the evening kick-off. Wiganers complain that the new ground isn't convenient, but it is if you're travelling by canal. If I'm coming back that way from a night match, I generally run into Andy Greg's diminutive brother, Bryn, biking his way along the towpath on his way to work.

* * *

We have another journey in mind; perhaps the most sentimental journey of the whole fortnight. Time was when walking up Wallgate and Standishgate brought a buzz with it, as though the whole town was drawn towards Central Park – and not just on match-days. Central Park did what it said on the can; if Wigan, with its chaotic redevelopment and labyrinthine one-way system, had a centre, this was it. People used to go down there and have a look at it and a walk around, even if there wasn't a match for weeks. Now that beating heart of the community is a Tesco car park. Just as well, I suppose, that it isn't a DIY superstore, otherwise I would have to tell that story about a passing motorist who stopped a Wiganer and asked: 'Is there a B&Q in Wigan?'

He put down his pie, scratched his head and went:

'A B&Q? Let's see . . . W . . . I . . . G . . .'

To lend a helping hand here, the correct answer is no. Nor is there an MFI in Hull or an M&S in Warrington, although there is a DFS in Huddersfield. Here in Wigan, there is some corner of a Tesco car park that is forever central to someone's career. One advantage of being not quite as prolific a loose-forward as Ellery Hanley is that you can remember most of your tries pretty clearly and Phil can certainly recall one he scored here in April 1991. 'It was the Championship decider against Widnes – 30,000 on. I'd just got into the side. I took the ball about here [at the back end of a Ford Mondeo] and flopped over in the corner about here [at the front end of the Ford Mondeo].' We all try to take up the same positions we occupied at that moment: Stevo roughly where the TV gantry would have been; me in the press box, which approximates now to a trolley corral; Uncle Bernard under the stand buying a pie; three or four of the others in primary school, although unfortunately not the one which used to overlook the ground. This time the try is acted out with more gusto. It has expanded into a 30-yard run through the cover defence of startled shoppers, followed by a dummy and a dart through a gap in a line of parked cars and a spectacular touchdown in a puddle. If we stay here another ten minutes, the scoring run will start somewhere up in the frozen foods section, with its towering cabinets of rock-hard pies. It's something that happens to tries as you get older; like the hairs in your ears, they grow longer and longer. That is not the end of the day's ceremonial, either, because there are balloons to be released. Unfortunately, they are released under the canopy at the front of the store, where they cluster, unwilling to come out into the drizzle, an appropriately half-cocked tribute to a place which used to mean so much and now just feels like a void.

* * *

We assemble again the following morning at Wigan North-Western Station, thinking that the sudden sacking of Stuart Raper might threaten the promised participation of the club in the next stage of the Trek. Not a bit of it; the man put in caretaker charge of the side, Mike Gregory, pulls off something of a public relations coup by insisting on the entire first team squad being there, each with a crisp, new tenner in hand. People often ask me, with ill-disguised envy, whether I get into matches free. Instead of my stock answer, which is to ask them whether they have to pay to get into their place of work, I can now honestly say that not only do I get in free to see Wigan, but that on occasion they also have to pay to come and see me.

Also there to meet us is the only man whose name comes close to that of George Orwell in terms of being synonymous with Wigan. Billy Boston has stuck around rather longer – 50 years at the last count – and is more usually bracketed with Eric Ashton than Eric Blair, as Orwell was christened, but they are surely somewhere up in the Wigan pantheon together. This book is not a survey of the playing achievements of everyone we met along the way, otherwise it would go on forever, but Billy's 478 tries for Wigan, combined with his charismatic personality, have made him the most enduringly famous figure in the game. He finished up at Blackpool, of course; even I wouldn't claim that he had his best years, or best weeks there, but I bet he had his own minibus. Billy won't be joining us on the walk. Like many of his contemporaries, his knees are shot – not helped by a hit-and-run incident a few years ago. It is said that the perpetrators of that crime, from which it was feared at the time that he would not recover, gave themselves up to the police when they realised what they had done, rather than face the wrath of a Wigan lynch mob.

A few weeks later, a couple of miles out of town, I was at another event which underlined Boston's legendary status – a gathering at Aspull Village Club to celebrate his half-century as a Wiganer. It was, apparently, exactly that long since his debut in an A-team game against Barrow – with 8,000 watching. The music for this bash was provided not by some local disco, but by Georgie Fame, who had flown in from a residency in New York. Apart from playing his hits and a range of jazz and blues standards – accompanied by his two sons, one playing drums in a Wigan shirt with 'Boston' across the back – Mr Fame read a poem he had written on the way up the motorway. It was somewhat in the dialect poetry tradition and the couplet that sticks with me was:

I come from a place nearby called Leigh,
Where we used to tremble at the name Billy B.

Clive Powell – because that's what he was called when one of my mates called Dave (how I wish some of us were called something more interesting) saw him in what he claims was his first paid gig, at Leigh Junior Supporters' Club Christmas Party – then made a shocking confession. He had left the tribe and deserted Leigh to watch Wigan, because Boston was there. It makes going on the road in your early teens backing Eddie Cochran and Gene Vincent, topping the charts around the world and marrying into the aristocracy – all of which he did – seem like minor lifestyle adjustments by comparison.

It was a convivial event, marred by just one jarring note – and not one from Mr Fame and Sons. Whilst there were plenty of people there from the rest of the rugby league world, there was no official representation from Wigan, the club for which, with all due respect to Blackpool Borough, he played all his meaningful rugby. Club and player have not always had an easy relationship since his retirement and I won't attempt to allocate blame here, but you can't help thinking how bloody typical it is of rugby league that two institutions like Wigan and Billy Boston, so overlapping and intertwined in the popular imagination, shouldn't be on speaking terms. Like many retirements, it hasn't been quite as big a success as his playing career, despite many years running The Griffin, the proximity of which to Central Park made it the town's busiest pub on match-days. One thing he can reflect upon is that he got out of there at the right time, because I doubt whether they do quite as well out of Tesco shoppers.

* * *

You just bump into rugby league in Wigan all the time. On our way back from Central Park, we come across Sean Long and Martin Gleeson, Wiganers both, even if they earn their wages down the road at St Helens. The next time I was at the station, I hopped into a taxi and found that it was driven by Graeme West, the former captain and coach of both Wigan and New Zealand. He finds it a lot less hassle than his last job in the game, coaching Chorley. If the weather's decent, he potters around all day and then drives until the work dries up in the early hours of the morning. He quite often picks up drunken youths who vaguely remember him playing, or coming to their school to present prizes – something he did a lot of – and who want to pay him ten times what it says on the meter. He just tells them to give him the right fare and not to spew up in the back. We have an illuminating chat about the ways in which various Wigan coaches, including him, have been sacked – the note on Eric Hughes' windscreen was a particularly stylish effort – and the perfidy of those who have done the sacking. I'm in as much of a quandary, however, as his regular clientele of tanked-up lads. I don't have a clue, any more than them, about the etiquette of tipping when you're in a taxi driven by one of your heroes.

On the day of the Trek, the presence of the whole Wigan squad adds to the sense of occasion. It had been a strange season up to this point, with injuries and departures leaving them with a distinctly threadbare look, but with the situation being redeemed by a clutch of graduates from Brian Foley's youth set-up. Brian, apart from being the sort of inexhaustible walker who puts me to shame, is one of the more remarkable men in the game. He was a village bobby in the shadow of Pendle Hill and once set up a highly successful kids' team in Nelson and Colne, consisting largely of Asian lads with no background in the game whatsoever, and financed by Brian's bare-knuckle prizefights against gypsies. They were winner-takes-all affairs, usually fought on riverbanks – away from the prying eye and the long arm of the law, except that he was the law – and he won enough of them to pay the costs of his team. He also once found a coven of witches sacrificing a lamb by the side of the road. You couldn't make up this sort of stuff.

Our route takes us past Wigan Pier, where you can be authentically bullied in a recreated Victorian classroom or have a look around Trencherfield Mill. That mill might be a museum piece now and most of its companions might be long closed down and demolished, but there is one mill in Wigan that still runs on a 24-hour shift pattern, with as much overtime as you can handle and no shut-down for Wakes weeks or bank holidays. It is the rumour mill and, like the giant Heinz factory but unlike Uncle Joe's Mint Balls, its products come in many varieties. All rugby league communities have an equivalent, but by comparison with Wigan, they are the mere branch offices of the central operation. As far as I can make out, this has always been the case; there would have been good rumours circulating around other clubs in the '50s and '60s, but the best of them would involve Billy Boston and his contemporaries. It just goes with the territory. Among more recent figures, Brett Kenny was one who seemed to attract the most bizarre stories. He played just one season for Wigan, arriving in the Orwellian year of 1984 and leaving soon after the unforgettable 1985 Cup final, but for the best part of a decade afterwards old men in mufflers and flat caps would lean over to you conspiratorially in the pie queue at Central Park or in some pub or club in town and say: 'Have you heard? Brett Kenny's back. My cousin saw him walking his dog by the canal.' It's the biggest tribute there can be, this sort of mythic immortality that keeps you in a town long after you've gone. Even when the news came that Raper was on his way out, the old ghost refused to be still. 'This coaching job . . .' said a bloke at the bar in The Swan and Railway, behind his hand. 'All decided . . . Take it from me . . . Brett Kenny.'

Another beauty I remember concerned Daryl Powell, in the days when he was a Great Britain centre or stand-off. One of my main sources of gossip at the time assured me that he had been to a garage in Wigan where they had been in the process of customising a club car with the legend: 'Daryl Powell, Wigan RLFC'. You can't get much more conclusive than that. Needless to say, it never happened, any more than Brett Kenny leading his dog down the towpath, but it was an appropriate episode to remember on this day, because we were about to get proof that the Wigan rumour mill is still capable of being cranked into throbbing, humming life – and that it is not always wrong.

In the summer of 2003, Powell was coaching Leeds and doing so with some success. They had reached the Challenge Cup final and had been top of Super League for most of the season – a lot better placed than Wigan, for instance. So when, as we were walking through Pemberton, someone rolled down the window of his passing car and shouted 'Have you heard about Leeds yet?' we thought nothing of it. But then someone on the top deck of a bus picked up the baton. 'Sacked Daryl Powell,' he yelled. 'That's right,' said a chap coming out of a *Wigan Observer* award-winning pie-shop. 'Tony Smith's taken over.' It was like a bad production of *Under Milk Wood*, in which the dramatis personae keep sticking their heads out of doors and windows to chime into the narrative.

It was a rumour with a particular Wigan resonance, because Smith had been one of the names linked with Raper's old job, and although it wasn't quite right, it wasn't wrong either. Powell was being moved upstairs at the end of the season, to become director of rugby – a title which can mean everything or nothing – with Smith coming in from Huddersfield to coach for two years, after which Powell would resume. As so often in rugby league, the truth was weirder than the rumour; I could just imagine Barrie McDermott's face when it was explained to him. It had to be Gary Hetherington's plan, in which case I was concerned that he might have got too much sun to his head a week or so earlier climbing up Lofthouse Hill out of Wakefield with us. It will probably turn out to be a masterstroke, but it was not well received that day on the shop floor of the rumour mill.

Although they play for a rival club, Denis Betts, promoted to assistant coach in Gregory's caretaker regime, has strong views on the jailing of Walker and Bailey. 'They talk about the jails overflowing and they put away lads who are basically good lads,' he says. Two of his own lads have, meanwhile, made good their own escape. Gareth Hock and Danny Tickle are reported to have been sighted nipping into a café for a bacon barm – at least, I'm pretty confident that's what they would have called them – before catching the number 28 bus back to the town centre. Someone says they were panicking a bit about missing their Open University course in existential philosophy, but that might just be a rumour. Even worse, Brian Carney and Adrian Lam cadge a lift in the local radio chap, Graham Lovett's, car without even bothering with a bacon barm. Heaven knows what an Irishman and a Papua New Guinean would have asked for and at least we'd already got their ten quids.

Up through Norley and Lamberhead Green and across the M6, we have diminishing numbers of Wigan players to keep us company. I confide to the proud Widnesian, Terry O'Connor, that for once in my life I'm looking forward to seeing his home town, which, after 220 miles, will look beautiful. He gives me the closest thing to a menacing glare that this most affable of players can manage and says: 'Widnes always looks beautiful.'

Soon we're in Orrell, which is a backwater of Wigan so posh that they play rugby union here. Inevitably, its club has been absorbed into the empire of Dave Whelan, who likes to hint from time to time that, if rugby league doesn't sort itself out and do things more in his way, well then, he has another code of rugby into which he might prefer to pour his largesse. When it still looked possible that Orrell might play their way into the Zurich Premiership, with its big wads of TV money for its member clubs, Wigan syphoned a few players off to their rugby union outpost – including Billy Boston's grandson, Wes Davies, and, briefly, Gary Connolly, before Leeds decided to offer him the chance to continue his league career. Turning left at Orrell Post, we are close enough to the ground for Uncle Bernard to smell the burnt-out clubhouse. I'm not accusing them of anything here, but the Orrell tie-in was one of the many things that Wigan fans didn't like and which contributed to their disillusionment with their club. If you imagine Wigan's fan-base at the start of the 1990s as a party in a very crowded room, then a few left early because winning every week was just too easy and predictable. Rather more departed when they stopped winning every week. There was a positive rush for the doors when they left Central Park and, when they couldn't win every week at a generally unloved new home, some more drifted off. Even in the 2003 season, when Wigan supporters were increasingly getting what they had always said they wanted – apart from the return of Brett Kenny – which was a team full of local kids, they were slow to be won back. I missed it, because I had made my Hock and Tickle-style escape in search of home comforts, but the evening at the JJB was the flattest of the whole trip, with an air of pessimism hanging over the place. It might have had a better feel to it after they embarked on a long unbeaten run under Gregory and Betts that took them into the Grand Final, but the hangover from their decade of domination of the game is that the Wigan public not only knows everything about rugby league and has heard, or possibly started, every rumour, but is also desperately hard to please.

There is such a welcoming committee outside Billinge Hospital that it seems only sensible to enquire whether they have a bed free for Stevo. Not at the moment, unfortunately, but I'm pretty sure we got him on some sort of waiting list. At the top of Billinge Hill there is a camera crew in Edwardian costume and a vintage car; just how long have we been on this walk? I'm reflecting on the fact that George Orwell was only 46 when he died in 1950, by which time he had not only fought in the Spanish Civil War and written *Animal*

Farm and *1984*, two books which are not quite as prophetic as they are cracked up to be, but which still haunt the popular imagination, he had also written *Down and Out in Paris and London*, with its uncannily accurate prediction of the teething pains during the difficult early seasons of Super League (Europe). I'm also told that he once wrote, in one of his memorable throw-away lines, that bombing the main stand at Twickenham would set back the cause of British Fascism by decades, but that is a quotation that my trawl through his work has failed to find. He got a bit of rugby into his repertoire, even if he never found the Pier and he never climbed Billinge Hill with sore feet.

X

St Helens: Viva Johnny Vegas

ONE OF THE RUNNING JOKES OF THE JOURNEY WAS THAT, BY spending four nights in the St Helens Hilton, we would probably break all records for duration of stay. The St Helens Hilton . . . it sounds about as likely as the Holiday Inn Featherstone or that popular all-in resort, Sandals Guantanamo Bay. Four nights there sounded like a long, long time. I couldn't have been more wrong; in fact, I'm thinking of going there for my holidays.

To get there, however, you have to negotiate your way through the divided community of Billinge. My predecessor on *The Independent* and, before that, the rugby league writer on the *Wigan Evening Post*, Paul Wilson, grew up here at Billinge Lower End, which is St Helens territory. 'You could get a bus to St Helens, but not to Wigan,' he recalls. At Billinge Higher End, the situation was reversed, because they looked towards Wigan. There has been a bit of seepage over the years, so that Wigan and Saints fans now live next door to each other in some confused parts of the village, but the old pattern still holds good. Pubs tend to be affiliated one way or the other. Wilson remembers one Boxing Day when, after a Saints victory over the old enemy, a predominantly Wigan pub was silenced by the brass band interrupting its Christmas carols to play 'When the Saints Go Marching In'. Andy Platt, the Saints and then Wigan forward, kept one of the pubs; the former landlord of another is in jail, not for switching clubs, but for the marginally more heinous crime of murdering his girlfriend, although the body has never been found.

Equally mysteriously, as we pass from Billinge Higher End to Billinge Lower End, the Wigan supporters who have been walking with us melt away like wraiths. At the parade of shops, they are miraculously replaced by Saints fans, including a gang of kids, resplendent in their replica kits, who are proudly staggering under the weight of about three tons of loose change, the proceeds of selling off their old toys and glasses of home-made lemonade. There is something very touching about this. Some of them might go to the school across the road, where Orrell St James – Andy Farrell's old club – now play their home games on the St Helens side of the demarcation line.

The lower end of Billinge peters out just before Carr Mill Dam and the East Lancashire Road . . . again. The late Harold Mather, when he was rugby league correspondent of what was then the *Manchester Guardian*, used to be justifiably proud of his address, one worthy of the Duke of Wellington or Ray Tennant: Number One, East Lancashire Road. That was up at Irlams o'th'Height and if you numbered it out continuously, we would be somewhere in the tens of thousands here, at the point where we cross over and into St Helens proper.

It's a strange place, with its own accent, its own sense of humour and, once upon a time, its own distinctive industry. St Helens was synonymous with glass; there are glassworks, not many of them still producing much glass, whichever way you go into the town centre. These were once mighty institutions in the sporting life of the town; for decades, Saints' true local derby was not against Wigan, but against St Helens – later Pilkington – Recs. In those works and still now in the town, they talked with their own version of a cut-glass accent. Snellensers, as they call them in Wigan, have a hint of Scouse about them, but they have their own sing-song intonation, which is hard to describe but impossible to mistake. Imagine Ray French going 'Why, oh why, oh why . . .' and you have the general flavour.

As for humour, St Helens people must surely have the same

problem with Johnny Vegas as we have in Bolton with Peter Kay. On the one hand, we take an almost proprietorial pride in the way he has tickled the nation's funny bone. On the other, and as the barman at my local puts it: 'Why should I pay good money to see him when I hear the same crap in here every night for nowt?' That, I suppose, is the danger in drawing with such wicked accuracy from your surroundings.

When you phone Saints' ground at Knowsley Road, you get Johnny Vegas on the other end. And not just a quick 'Thank you for phoning St Helens', either; you get a full cabaret turn about life being all about choices and the club shop not selling milk and bread. If you have cause to phone the club regularly, you get to understand what the barman at The Ainsworth means about the over-familiarity of local humour. We invited Michael Pennington – as Mr Vegas, the most famous non-rugby league playing Snellenser since Sir Thomas Beecham, was christened – on the Trek, but he was in London, waiting for his wife to give birth. Another flimsy excuse, but you can't really knock a man who turns down an offer from *Hello!* magazine and instead sells his wedding pictures to *Viz* for £1. I finally ran him to ground in his London hotel, from which he was doing promotional interviews for his new film, *Sex Lives of the Potato Men*.

Perversely, but in exactly the way I have seen it affect other exiles, rugby league and Saints have become more important to him as he has spent less time in the town. 'I need to sort out my fixture list. If ever I get a job up North, they're playing the Broncos down here.'

As Michael Pennington, he used to shin over the wall to watch Mal Meninga – 'the David Beckham of his day', he calls him. 'Now I get in for nowt, that's the main difference. But I don't want to be Elton John, or the number one fan or anything like that. The real fans are the ones who pay their money.

'But if I can help them in any way, during the short time I'll be around, I will. I'm only the blink of an eye. They'll be around a lot longer than I will.'

From a distance, the importance of the club to the town is also more obvious to him. 'It's the focal point for pride in the town,' he says. 'The industry's gone; it's only the rugby that's not let us down.'

He went to rugby union-playing schools, but trained at Saints with the Under 15s. 'But it was my brother, Mark, who was the good player in the family. He was in the same year as Bernard Dwyer. They were the two best players, but Mark didn't pursue it. He used to take me out training every Sunday, but training usually meant him running at me.'

He has done his best to keep up the family connection by taking his six-year-old nephew to matches, when life as Johnny Vegas has permitted. 'He told me on the way in that he preferred football, but he loved it. He knows more than I do about it now. He looks at me like I'm talking out of my arse.'

* * *

St Helens' glassy heritage is all too transparent as you come into town. The compulsory Wetherspoons is called The Glasshouse, the compulsory monument to a bygone industry is The World of Glass, which was voted Best Small Visitor Attraction in England 2002 – no doubt by thousands of well-satisfied small visitors. Even the Safeway supermarket has an exuberant, thrusting glass pinnacle, and The Hilton is a symphony in glass.

As I admitted earlier, I was not much looking forward to four nights – the best part of a week out of your life – under its glazed roof, or anywhere else in St Helens, for that matter. Inside the hotel, though, you're in a different world, all filtered sunlight and blonde wood. It feels so redolent of the southern hemisphere that you could imagine looking out onto Manly beach or Auckland harbour. It does indeed have a water view of sorts – onto the branch canal from the glassworks across the road. This little finger of water and weeds is known as Hotties, because it was used to channel water, heated by the glassmaking process, away from the works. Even now, it's warm enough to support some exotic species of fish amongst the algae, the empty bottles and the inevitable supermarket trolleys. From inside The Hilton, it looks perfectly pleasant.

The place has other virtues as well. It's the first place I've stayed at since my granny's in Derbyshire where you get a matronly hug at breakfast. Admittedly, the main recipient was Stevo – something of a regular at the establishment – but, if you are in the vicinity, you get one too. Nor is it the case, as I had assumed, that nobody stays there very long. Sure enough, they get their share of glass-related business traffic passing through swiftly before dashing back to Dusseldorf or Strasbourg by the weekend, but it's also where St Helens put their overseas players until they find a house. Sean Hoppe was a popular long-term resident, but it is the stay of Darrell Trindall that is most vividly remembered. The temperamental Australian half-back was one of Ellery Hanley's signings for the 1999 season, but he left, without playing a Super League match, after a string of 'incidents' which set the rumour mills humming from Haresfinch to Clock Face. Our team-member, Adam, was at The Hilton – waiting for Marie to finish her shift at the health club, where the likes of Ray French and Austin Rhodes bask like Roman generals reliving old campaigns – the night that 'Tricky' Trindall, as he was known, demolished a wall with his car. Typically, for such a laid-back management – that's The Hilton, not St Helens – they didn't make much of a fuss about it. They were thinking of moving it anyway and they have since replaced it with a flower-bed and a fence. Adam showed it to us and we all agreed it was an improvement.

They have other distinguished guests as well. One night we were there, the bar filled up late with the personnel of a rock tour. I wouldn't have recognised him, but the main man was one of the Goss brothers, who made up the briefly mega-huge Bros in the 1980s. Apparently, there is a good Goss Bros and a bad Goss Bros. I think this one was Luke, but it could have been Matt. Anyway, he was definitely the good Goss, because he left his entourage of roadies and groupies to come over and shake hands. 'You're doing it for charity, man . . .' he said. 'That's beautiful, man.' He became an even better Goss when he sent over not only a donation, but also a bottle of champagne. Champagne with rock gods – well, rock demi-gods – in the St Helens Hilton; this is living in the fast lane, or perhaps simply in the wrong lane, as Darrell Trindall discovered when he hit that wall.

It wasn't all rock 'n' roll in St Helens, of course; you couldn't keep up that pace indefinitely. There was, by way of contrast, the night we were invited for a meal at an old folk's home up Elephant Lane. This is a famous thoroughfare and not just in St Helens – thanks to the promotional work of Roy Haggerty. The Saints and Great Britain second-rower was on tour in Australia, the story goes, and was asked at some official reception where he came from.

'England,' he replied, truthfully.

'Yes, mate, we sort of figured that. But whereabouts in England?'

'Top of Elephant Lane,' says Roy.

At least, that's the story as I've always known it; there is another version which makes marginally more sense. It runs like this.

Australian (let's make him a high-powered diplomat): 'And where are you from, Mr Haggerty?'

Roy: 'Thatto Heath.'

Australian: 'And where, pray, is that?'

Roy: 'Top of Elephant Lane.'

Thatto Heath, which produced Alex Murphy as well as Roy Haggerty, is indeed at the top of Elephant Lane, not far from our evening venue, where, having declined the liquidised food option, we dine handsomely in preparation for the rigours of the following morning. That sees us set off from the steps of St Helens Town Hall, in the company of the club mascot, St Bernard, and a couple of very high-quality injured players, Paul Sculthorpe and Chris Joynt. Scully is recuperating from the hamstring injury that hampered him through the second half of the season. Joynt is convalescing after a clean-up operation on his knee. That, as we head off down Parr Street, brings back memories of his last major bout of knee trouble. It was during the 1996 Lions tour to New Zealand and, just by co-incidence, I had a similar problem myself at the time. I thought the best contribution I could make to the British cause was to be Joynty's training partner as he tried to get himself ready for action. If nothing else, it should have boosted his confidence. Unfortunately, I made rather better progress than he did, so that when the Great Britain coach, Phil Larder, came to check on us after our latest session of underwater running, he got the news he didn't want to hear. 'Well, Phil, I've got bad news and good news,' said Doc Zaman – at least I thought it was Doc Zaman; the physio, Alan

Tomlinson, says it was him. 'Chris Joynt is still struggling. But I think Hadfield's going to be OK.' Do you know, that hardly cheered him up at all. He could be a dour man, Phil Larder; I wonder what happened to him.

Far more disturbing than that memory is the way that, for the first time on the Trek, we are, judging by the position of the sun, heading due east, back towards Hull rather than onwards, ever onwards to Widnes. It's the need to backtrack to Warrington that is responsible, but the psychology of it is very, very bad. St Helens, as its neighbours never tire of reminding it, is not in Lancashire, or even in Greater Manchester, like Wigan; it is not even, like Warrington and Widnes, in Cheshire. It is, if you accept these borders at all, in Merseyside – and that is something which has influenced the club's thinking in recent years. It is surrounded on its three other sides by other rugby league clubs, so if it is to broaden its base, it has to look west – towards the city of Liverpool. When David Howes was in charge, they played one game a season at Anfield – and drew reasonable crowds there. The new regime at Knowsley Road have launched a campaign called Saints and the City, through which they hope to win Liverpudlian hearts and minds. It is a hard sell, because Liverpool is more obsessed with football to the exclusion of all else than even Manchester, but it has to be worth a try. A couple of months after the Trek, I went to one of their bashes in Liverpool, at the top of the tower in the St John's Centre, looking down on the floodlit Liver Building, the two cathedrals and the Mersey. It used to be a revolving restaurant, but it proved a little expensive for local tastes and it revolves no more, although you can achieve very much the same effect by turning around very slowly yourself, disconcerting though that might be for whoever you are talking to. They attracted a good number of the city's movers and shakers for wine and canapés and a chance to chat with Paul Sculthorpe and Keiron Cunningham. If the object of the exercise was to convince you that you should get your company involved with Saints, then it would have been hard not to be impressed, especially in the light of all the development work the club is doing on Merseyside. There are a number of born-and-bred Scousers working their way through the Saints' age-group sides.

The most startling revelation, however, came from the man from Gillette, who came up with this truly outstanding nugget of trivia: the man who fronted up the first 'Best a man can get' shaving advert was Tom Van Vollenhoven's son! It was worth going just for that and it tied in with a story Alex Murphy, Saints' greatest-ever half-back, had told about Voll, its greatest winger, a few days earlier.

Apparently, the young Murphy had found out that Vollenhoven, most unusually for the time, was being paid by Saints in the summer as well as during the season. He went to see the chairman, Harry Cook, and told him he wanted the same arrangement.

'But Alex,' he said, 'you're not as good a player as Tom Van Vollenhoven.'

'I am during the bloody summer!'

Still intoxicated by the Chateau Scouse, the smoked salmon and the views of the Wirral, I was enthusing about Saints' enterprise to a chum a few days later. 'It's all very well,' he said. 'But what happens when they get them back to Knowsley Road.' It's a fair point, because Saints' famous old ground is becoming a bit of an albatross around their necks. It has always had its quirks, like the way the back of the stand is cut away to accommodate a long closed railway line and an away dressing-room so small that some visiting players had to change in the corridor, but, until recently, it didn't feel like a bad place to be. Now, by comparison with what is happening elsewhere, particularly down the road in Warrington, it feels like being in a museum. 'It's a bit disgraceful that we could finish up being the best club with the worst ground,' as Johnny Vegas puts it rather elegantly. The club had hopes of building a new stadium, on – inevitably – an old glassworks site, not far from our way out of town, but it fell through for want of planning permission. That new regime at Saints, headed by financial heavy hitters like Eamonn McManus and Sean McGuire, who feel thoroughly at home with city slickers in the Merseyside moonlight, know they have to sort this out if they are to dig the club out of its fiscal hole. Hang on, you might be saying at this stage, aren't Saints the most successful club of the Super League era, as they reminded us a few dozen times that night in Liverpool? Indeed they are, but that is traditionally a double-edged sword. Over the last quarter of a century, every club that has achieved sustained success has done so at the cost of financial meltdown a little further down the line. It happened to both the Hull clubs, to Widnes, to Wigan, even to Halifax after their little flurry and – without them really having the success as the scene-setter – to Leeds. Only Bradford have so far broken free of the syndrome of success today, misery tomorrow. It works on a smaller scale as well. The biggest cause of financial crises at clubs further down the pecking order is winning too many games and having to pay out too much winning money to their players. It's the contradiction at the heart of the professional game.

* * *

You could not have a better native guide to St Helens than Ray French, because just about every brick comes, for him, with a story attached. That is true in a couple of senses of a block of nondescript low-rise flats we walk past. When he was at Leeds University, Ray spent his holidays hod-carrying on the site. One day, when they were almost finished, the man in charge of the project came around to the site, turned pale and said: 'Bloody hell! You've built them the wrong way round.' Sure enough, someone had reversed the plans and nobody had noticed until now, when it was far too late to do anything about it. When you look at the flats carefully, you can see that there is something wrong. The front elevation, facing onto the street, looks suspiciously like a back view and, if you peer around the back, there are neat little front porches jutting into the back yards. As we wandered past, 40-odd years later, they finally seem to have decided to do something about it, because the flats are boarded up, apparently awaiting demolition. Or maybe some genius is going to turn them around.

A little further on, just past Blackbrook's ground, where a young Gary Connolly, among many, many others, learned to play, there is a culverted stream feeding into the Sankey Brook. When Ray was a little lad, the highlight of Sunday mornings used to be coming down here and watching the colliers – St Helens was important for coal as well as glass – racing the little wooden boats they had made. It might sound like a childish hobby, but it was in deadly earnest; they used to work all week on tiny modifications which might make the foot-long craft go that little bit faster, the water conditions were studied with an expert eye and there used to be serious money riding on the outcome. It was something I'd never heard of elsewhere, but the general idea of it rang a bit of a bell, because wherever there were miners they seemed to devise some form of competition, usually something they could bet on. In Westleigh, when I knocked around there, they had a patch of land called the piggy field, where they had played what was once a common northern game of hitting a little slug of wood – the piggy – as far as you could with a pick-axe handle. I never saw parring, in which men in clogs kicked each other in the shins until one collapsed – and I still can't see how it would ever have taken more than one kick – although I saw some amateur rugby league games that came close to the same ethos. Slightly more civilised were the nude foot-races on Whitworth Moor that survived, despite attempts to suppress them, well into the last century.

Perhaps inspired by memories of successful betting coups on the little boats of his youth, Ray makes a rather rash wager as we walk towards Newton-le-Willows. It's been a bee in his bonnet for some time, this 'momentum rule' that Stevo is always banging on about in his Sky commentaries. 'No such thing,' Frenchie says. 'Doesn't exist. A thousand quid says it doesn't exist.' Admittedly, the way Stevo describes it, it does sound unlikely. 'Look, it's quite simple,' he says whenever anyone asks him to explain it, which is regrettably often. 'If I get thrown out of a train as it goes through Dewsbury, I might hit the ground in Batley, but I've still gone backwards.'

Contrary to popular opinion, it is not his invention. It's a hobby-horse of Neville Smith, who, before he was Sky's rugby league producer, did a fair bit of refereeing in his native Australia. He still keeps a rule-book on his desk and all it takes is a phone call to him and a fax to the St Helens Hilton and the proof is there. Rather than extract the full £1,000 from a man who is now down to his last three or four jobs, it is agreed that most of that sum will be waived in return for a command performance of some of Ray's great commentary moments, later that day in Warrington town centre. It drew quite a little crowd when he launched into such old favourites as: 'Why, oh why, oh why has he done that? That's why', and 'He's going for the line! Has he got the legs?', not forgetting 'Andy Gregory – he's a cheeky, chirpy chappie'. Ray has never spawned a nationwide imitation industry quite on the scale that Eddie Waring did, but wherever rugby league people are gathered together, someone will have a stab at his distinctive St Helens patois, especially if Ray happens to be there to shake his head at the childishness of it all.

Our route, the wrong way out of St Helens, follows the Sankey Valley, which now has a pleasant walkway alongside what was the first navigation – or canalised river – of the Industrial Revolution. It's another area of notable firsts, this; a couple of miles to the south is Rainhill, where *The Rocket*, built by George Stephenson, emerged as the winner of the steam engine trials of 1830. Even closer is Burtonwood, which was the biggest American airbase in Europe during the Second World War, hence the local popularity of chewing-gum and even baseball. It still has some of its old hangars, near a service area on the M62, but it is a stretch of land which has been looking for a use ever since hostilities ceased. Despite it being rather closer to the centre of St Helens than to the centre of Warrington, the Wolves, under the stewardship of Peter Deakin, had plans to build their new stadium out here in this no-man's-land. Looking north, there is the grandstand of the thriving racecourse at Haydock, cunningly sited where the M6 meets the East Lancs. They have a rugby league club at Haydock as well and they are there in force to meet us at the road junction in Earlstown. It is one of the lump-in-throat moments of the trip, because, apart from the Haydock Under 9s, glowing in their freshly laundered kit, there is Luke Bryan and his mum. Luke broke his neck playing for the club several years ago and is now quadriplegic and confined to a wheelchair. I know Phil has been a source of help and encouragement to them since his own, infinitely less debilitating playing injury, but for them to take the trouble to come out and see us is deeply moving – and a reminder of the heavy price a few individuals pay for all the pleasure the rest of us have had from this game.

Newton-le-Willows is one of those places which, close though it is to my base, I had never really looked at. It has a broad, handsome main street that teeters on the edge of being quite elegant. It doesn't feel the least bit like rugby league territory, but Colin Welland recalls growing up here and feeling completely surrounded by the game. Go a couple of miles in any direction and you're in the heartlands of – going clockwise – Saints, Wigan, Leigh, Warrington or Widnes. It's the Luxembourg of rugby league – not anywhere itself, but near everywhere that is.

It's the Warrington frontier we're heading for, but, before we get there, a passing car skids to an abrupt halt and one of the most recognisable figures in the game jumps out. I hadn't seen Doug Laughton since he finished his stint at Widnes, by which time he was starting to look old and tired as he brewed up for you in his little office in the now demolished pavilion. Now he looks tanned and fit, like a 35-year-old; a 35-year-old who has had a fairly hard life, but still dramatically rejuvenated. The last time I saw Dougie by the side of a road, it was on the way to a match at Workington, where he had the whole of the first team squad walking down the hard shoulder to get the travel-stiffness out of their limbs. He always had his own way of doing things, but we will rarely see a more entertaining team than the one he built through his daring raids on rugby union for the likes of Martin Offiah – whose nickname of 'Chariots' derived from Welland's Oscar-winning film – Jonathan Davies and Alan Tait. They won the World Club Challenge one unforgettable night at Old Trafford and even held up the Wigan juggernaut for a while. After that, of course, they went bust, in the traditional manner. I don't imagine Doug was the most cost-conscious coach in the game or the most technical, but, by God, his teams played the game like they enjoyed it.

XI

Warrington: Gateway to the South

THE 'WELCOME TO WARRINGTON' SIGN WE PASS ON THE A49 reveals that the town is twinned with the region of Nachod in the Czech Republic. Apparently, the stress should be on the second syllable, making it Na-HODD, but I'll take a lot of convincing that it shouldn't be pronounced Knackered.

Past Winwick Hospital, once the largest mental institution in the area, before the Government hit on the alternative strategy of turning out its inmates to wander around bus stations – Care in the Community, they called it – we cross the M62 for the last time. Junction 9 is a particularly evocative one for me, because of the spectacular scale of the queue you have to negotiate to turn off here on Sunday afternoons. To the uninitiated, it can seem as though a remarkably massive rugby crowd is heading for Wilderspool; the truth is far, far sadder. Not long after the motorway roundabout, most of the traffic turns right. These glum men behind their steering wheels are not going to the match, as nature dictates they should be; they are taking their wives, girlfriends or mothers-in-law to IKEA. It is the most depressing sight in the world; they look like the demoralised remnants of a vanquished and enslaved nation, being dragged off to be paraded in shame through the streets of Rome. Even worse than that is the occasional glimpse of a man who seems genuinely enthusiastic about the prospect – a member of the

Warrington chapter of the Stepford Husbands, all trembly with excitement about stripped pine and soft furnishings when there is a rugby league team down the road, ready to bash itself and its opposition senseless, that needs his support. As the sage Alistair Cooke – he of a million *Letters From America* – once observed: 'I have a deep unspoken pity for people who have no attachment to a single sport. I am almost as sorry for them as I am for teetotallers.'

When they get to IKEA, this captive tribe should stop at the mirror department, take a long, hard look at themselves and ask how it ever came to this, how we could have allowed shopping to become this country's main leisure pursuit. It is madness, as they would have said at Winwick, but I speak as one whose only trip to that other shrine to shopping, the Trafford Centre, was for a Challenge Cup draw – a record I hope to maintain. Mind you, I hear the reindeer balls at IKEA are pretty good.

On rereading the last two paragraphs, I can see that they could be misinterpreted as just a shade misogynist, so let me just say that I feel equally sorry for any women dragged shopping by their menfolk, for men forced to go there by other men and by women coerced by other women. This is an equal opportunities rant.

* * *

Warrington is quite different in atmosphere from its rugby league-playing neighbours. Apart from the spectacular display of pipes, spouts and valves that welcomes you into Bank Quay Station, the centre of the town is less obviously industrial and it has certainly been less reliant on a single industry. Before they became the Wolves, the rugby league team were known – and still are in strictly fundamentalist circles – as the Wire. But wire-making was only part of the commercial picture, rather than the whole story. There is not even a museum devoted to it; there is no Wonderful World of Wire anywhere to be seen and the Wetherspoons isn't called The Wirepullers, so it can't have been that crucial. What Warrington was really famous for was beer; at one time, there were more pints produced here than in the even more famous brewing centre of Burton upon Trent. These days, Greenall Whitley consists largely of expensive flats overlooking the Ship Canal and the Wire/Wolves are about to move into their new stadium on the site of the old Peter Walker brewery. They brewed the beer of my blissful youth here, not to mention the beer of a moderately contented early middle age, until they were shut down by Carlsberg-Tetley – an act of vandalism for which, I fear, no amount of Super League sponsorship will ever fully compensate.

The new ground, imaginatively named the Halliwell Jones Stadium, after the sponsoring car dealership, is to the north of the town centre, so it is an obvious stopping-off place. The Lord Rodney, almost next door, is a popular luncheon spot for workers on the site. From the outside, it looks to be taking shape quite impressively, but one chap, in his hard hat and boots, tells a different story: 'The pitch is so full of crap we have to go on it in wellies and all the building is cheap and rubbish.' Nice when you can take a pride in your work. One thing the HJS does have, like Halifax, is standing terraces, something we might have thought we had seen the last of at newly built stadia. With no plans to play league football there, however, there is no reason why not – and rugby league fans prefer it when they have somewhere to stand. The other great bonus is that it is right in the town centre, not out in the middle of nowhere – like Burtonwood. I can see it having plenty of atmosphere, although whether it will ever be quite as intimidating as a packed Wilderspool is debatable.

Warrington's historic home is on the other side of the town centre, past the statue of Oliver Cromwell, along Wilderspool Causeway and over the Mersey, which, more often than it does now, used to foam with the soap that was another local product. It was never the most beautiful of grounds, even before the building and, some years later, the closure of the snooker club along one touchline that made it effectively three-sided. In the days when they still bothered to clean them, the floor-to-ceiling windows at Snookers did have their uses. From the opposite side of the ground, they acted as a mirror so that you could see what was happening on the blind side of the scrum – and, this being Warrington, it was usually something that shouldn't have been. Visiting players used to call Wilderspool 'The Zoo', in recognition of the warm welcome they could expect from opponents and spectators alike. Warrington have had their share of gifted players, including arguably the greatest winger ever to play the game, but when I sift my memories of Wilderspool they all have an undercurrent of violence running through them: Paul Cullen and Andy Goodway fighting in the tunnel; the exploits of the pack that included the likes of Dave Chisnall and Mike Nicholas. Or the week that the then chairman, Peter Higham, signed Les Boyd, Kevin Tamati and Alan Rathbone – three pantomime villains if ever there were and surely a case of over-egging the intimidating forward pudding. 'We aren't expecting all three of them to be available very often,' he said, philosophically. Had they been, there would have been a prima facie case for accusing the disciplinary committee of dozing off on the job.

Despite, or perhaps because of its bloodthirsty associations, Warrington fans were deeply attached to Wilderspool. The club has softened the blow of leaving the old place by doing so in easy stages, with a series of 'final' matches reminiscent of Frank Sinatra's commercially shrewd ploy of spending his last 30 years on 'farewell' tours. This was a considerate policy on Warrington's part, because nobody wanted a repeat of those scenes of emotional devastation that disfigured the last game at Central Park, a ground that Wigan made the mistake of leaving just the once. By way of spreading the pain as thinly as possible, Warrington had a last Super League game against Wakefield, followed by a last game against New Zealand A. Even when Wilderspool staged its last-ever (and first-ever) European Nations Cup final between England A and France, it was a case not so much of goodbye as of au revoir, because they still had a last game against Penrith Under 18s, followed by a couple of farewell appearances by the local amateurs, Woolston Rovers, not to mention three Christmas friendlies. There has not been anything milked dry with such enthusiasm since the Co-op Dairy closed, although they missed a trick by not selling a special season ticket covering the whole long farewell. Even the ground announcer – one of a breed who can normally be relied upon to toe the party line – was taking the piss by the time of the England–France adieu. 'Thank you for attending this last game at Wilderspool,' he said. 'We look forward to seeing you at the next last game at Wilderspool.'

When Brian Bevan played his last game at Wilderspool, it really was his last – apart from one appearance in a testimonial Sevens for his namesake, John Bevan, a couple of decades later. After his official farewell, he went off to Blackpool Borough and it doesn't come much more final than that. There has simply never been a winger like Brian Bevan, the cadaverous, strapped-up Australian who scored 796 tries in Britain. He became one of the very select band of players to have his statue erected near the scene of his glories – Wally Lewis at Lang Park is another – when they put up a set of goalposts and his likeness, in full flight, on the roundabout near the ground. There were moves afoot to transport it to the new ground, where it would instantly confer a patina of history on the new metal and concrete, but Clarrie Owen, the Warrington stalwart who knew Bevan throughout his career with the club, told me he was dead against that idea. He promised Bev's widow it would stay where it is and, as far as he's concerned, that is where it should stay – even if the roundabout only leads in future to a soulless little housing development on the site of the old ground, probably with a token Brian Bevan Avenue and a Harry Bath Crescent. If there are any houses for rent there and the occupants ever fall into arrears, I trust they will be issued with a final demand, followed by a final, final demand and a really definitely final demand. That would be in keeping with the ground's latter-day traditions.

Long before the county boundaries went walkabout, and Warrington was still officially in Lancashire, it still felt like it had more in common with towns to the south, rather than to the north. Long before it was lumped in with Cheshire, it already resembled a bigger version of some of that county's market towns more than it did Wigan or Bolton. There is a good deal of fake half-timbering and even some that could be genuine. The old coat of arms of the town included the flag of Cheshire as well as that of Lancashire and, by the time you are through Stockton Heath, you are into classic Cheshire villages like Daresbury, birthplace of Charles Lutwidge Dodgson, a writer of mathematical treatises, better known for his other works under the pen name of Lewis Carroll.

Town-twinning is a funny business – Stevo discovered on this trek that Dewsbury doesn't have a twin town, but it does have a suicide pact with Cleckheaton – but Warrington could as well be paired with Knutsford as Knackered. The real proof that it is on the wrong side of the Mersey, however, is outside the Town Hall.

If you judge towns by their Town Halls, then we have been through some places with some pretty big ideas of themselves. I have a particular soft spot for Leeds', which is a big, squarer, but not quite as well proportioned version of Bolton's and indeed Plymouth's, as civic authorities sometimes bought designs which were being simultaneously built elsewhere; Town Halls off the peg. It can lead to confusion. Many years ago, I was dozing on the settee (not IKEA) in front of the television when Sir Francis Chichester was sailing into his home port of Plymouth after his single-handed voyage around the world. I woke with a start to see him passing what appeared to be Bolton Town Hall and thought: 'Bloody hell! The sea-crazed old coot has taken a wrong turn and gone up the Croal.'

Warrington's equivalent is the first on the route which looks like an elegant country house, because, until the town swallowed it up, that is what it was. The owner, a Colonel John Wilson Patten, sold it to the council in 1870, because the expanding industrial area of the town had encroached on his privacy. In fact, it had just about got him fenced in, although not entirely with wire. They bought Bank Hall, as it was known, for £9,000, and got the 13 acres of parkland surrounding it thrown in. Built in the 1750s, it had once enjoyed uninterrupted views to the Mersey and the Cheshire countryside beyond. The first owner, Thomas Patten, had made the Mersey navigable as far as Warrington, so that he could preside as the merchant controlling much of the distribution of the goods imported up the river. In a way, that is what Warrington still does, now distributing everything from coils of wire to IKEA rugs via a motorway system which could have been built with the town's interests in mind. No wonder that it has been less vulnerable to the fluctuations of a dominant industry than other rugby league towns; there will always be stuff to be shifted, even in an age when people might order it over the internet. Warrington's key position in the transport infrastructure also means that people can live there and work pretty much anywhere in the north-west. The new town that sprawls to its east is full of people whose social and sporting roots are elsewhere, notably in Manchester and Liverpool. There are days when, apart from the traffic jams of shoppers, there are other queues leaving town for Anfield and Old Trafford.

Back at the Town Hall, there was still something missing until in 1893 a councillor named Frederick Monks saw a magnificent set of gilded gates at a foundry in Ironbridge. Being a director of the foundry in which he found them, he was able to offer them as a gift to Warrington; they were worth accepting for the story attached, if for nothing else. They had been made in Coalbrookdale for the International Exhibition in London in 1862 and the plan after that was to present them to Queen Victoria to be used at the newly purchased property at Sandringham in Norfolk. First of all, Her Majesty had to check them over and, for that purpose, they were erected in Rotten Row in Hyde Park. Unfortunately, Victoria saw them in juxtaposition with a nearby statue of Oliver Cromwell, modelled by the same artist who put the figures of the Greek goddess of victory – called Nike, before the sportswear company pinched the name – on top of the gates. That was enough to turn her against them – strange how people resent those who have decapitated their predecessors – and she rejected them out of hand. Sandringham's loss was Warrington's gain, because, after 30 years of lying around unwanted, they were officially opened – what else would you want to do with gates? – in that most pivotal of years, 1895.

Now, that statue of Cromwell looks out into the sporadically soapy Mersey, but the gates themselves form one of the more remarkable sights in Rugby League Land, right up there with the Humber Bridge, the Piece Hall, Wainhouse's Folly and Stevo's expenses. They would look more at home in Versailles than in industrial Lancashire and I remember the eyes of some of Warrington's overseas players – like Allan Langer, about the size of one of the Greek goddesses – open wide when the club held its pre-season bash at the Town Hall a few years ago. Although I doubt whether this was in the mind of Councillor Monks when he rescued them from obscurity in Shropshire, they also formed an impressive backdrop to the start of the last day of the Trek.

By this stage, the daily workload had shrunk to manageable proportions. The mileage was no longer daunting and, whilst Billinge Hill had not exactly been massive, it had been notable as the last one we would have to climb. From here, it was a mere stroll into Widnes and we had plenty of company. Warrington supporters were out in force, many of them still shaken by the news about one of their old heroes. Tawera Nikau had played with great distinction and success in three countries: his native New Zealand; with Cronulla in Australia; and, most of all, with a series of clubs, including York, Sheffield and Castleford, in the north of England. His last British club was Warrington, for whom he played in his typically dashing style at loose-forward in 2000 and 2001; he might even have been there the day we marvelled at those gates, I can't really remember. I always felt I knew him a little better after meeting him on his home turf of Huntly, a closed-down coal-mining town on the North Island of New Zealand that struck me at the time as the Featherstone of the Southern Hemisphere, although that rather downplays Featherstone's charms and amenities. He achieved a hell of a lot after playing his way out of that hick town, but his time at Warrington and in England ended in tragedy. One day, he came home from the club and discovered that his wife, Letitia, a fiercely intelligent lawyer who was, in many ways, the driving force behind him, had hung herself. Somehow, he held things together for the kids and even played a few games to round off his time with Warrington before heading home. Now we heard that 'T' – as he was generally known – had been in a motorbike accident and had lost a leg. Here was someone we all felt we knew, whose life seemed to be turning into a badly written melodrama. There was an undertow of sympathy and concern for him throughout that day, laced with a slight tinge of hysteria at the quotes from his doctors, which had gone out through the agencies and appeared in several papers. They were delighted with his progress after his operation, they said, and hoped to soon have him back on his feet. I need hardly add that nobody actually laughed, but rugby league's affinity with black humour – even when it is inadvert – would not entirely be denied, even at a time like this. If one person suggested that we should hold a fund-raising walk for Tawera, then fifty must have done, and yet every one of them knew that it was a suggestion loaded with irony; but a lap of his British clubs, or even Huntly to Featherstone, for the more ambitious walker . . . it has a certain attraction.

As we walked, I realised that I was experiencing a greater kinship than usual with Warrington supporters. It could have had something to do with the T-shirt. The previous evening, Mr Stephenson had, in his generous way, presented me with a Man of the Tour award. I don't know what I'd done to deserve it, apart from turning up and keeping going, but I said then that it would go into my crowded rugby league trophy cabinet, along with my Pennine League Division Six winners' medal from the 1983–84 season with Prestwich and some Clubman of the Year bauble from Bolton a couple of years later. It might sound ungrateful, but after all this time I can admit that I've never really been keen on that 'clubman' business, not by comparison with the sunlit pinnacle of achievement that is being named Player of the Year. It's a bit of a sympathy vote, a bit like being a teenager and the girl you fancy telling you that she really, really likes you, but not in that way. As it turned out, I had need for my new award immediately, because the one great, universal truth of touring is that you can't have too much kit and certainly not too many T-shirts; I must have got through a dozen that day in Bradford alone. I wasn't even worried about the printing on it. Based on some trumped-up snoring charge, Stevo had wanted to adorn it with 'The Wildebeest'. For some reason – economising on the lettering, perhaps, or simply the inability to spell it – this was abbreviated to 'Wilders' and that, combined with the primrose and blue colour scheme, must have made it look as though I was pledging allegiance to their soon-to-be-former ground and all it stood for. It was a lot less popular in Widnes, where small children hissed and aged crones gave me the evil eye, but those were pleasures that lay a few miles ahead.

* * *

Apart from the road we are walking along, over Sankey Brook and through Penketh, Warrington and Widnes are linked by a canal running parallel to the Mersey, another claimant to being the first of its type. I walked it once when I had a few hours to kill before a match and, for the connoisseur of industrial dereliction, there is truly nowhere like it. The abandoned works at the Widnes end, in particular, would be the perfect film set for a documentary about the end of the world. Sandwiched between canal and river, just before Fiddler's Ferry power station – another holiday brochure name, if ever there was one – there is the site of the actual ferry that used to run across to the apparently empty Cheshire side. You would wonder about the demand for such a service, even a couple of hundred years ago, but it used to do a lively trade with spectators on their way to bare-knuckle fights, which were illegal on the Lancashire side, but tolerated on the Cheshire bank. If Brian Foley had been born a couple of centuries earlier, this is where he would have earned his supplementary income. If you turn away from the cooling towers and towards the marina, it can be a surprisingly seductive spot on a sunny afternoon, with the sail-boats scudding past on the Mersey – but no ferries full of fight fans.

Back on the road, it is Stevo's good fortune to be walking with Warrington's noisiest fans – the little gang of drummers who beat out their merry tattoo throughout matches at Wilderspool. Some new grounds have banned such expressions of enthusiasm, so their status might be in some jeopardy at the new stadium, but anyone prepared to lug the big bass drum, which must weigh a good 50lb, from Warrington to Widnes will not be silenced easily. As they walk along with Stevo, there are, admittedly, a few complaints about the dull, monotonous racket, the banging on interminably to the same old tune. Some people don't much care for the drumming either.

Just past the power station – impressive in scale even after all the others we've seen – is Cuerdley Cross, one of the natural dividing lines between rival clubs. There are dozens of Widnes fans waiting here outside the pub, not quite willing to venture any closer to Warrington. In a remarkable display of integration, however, they mix in with the primrose and blue throng. Joan West, a Warrington fan of mature years who had been there at Hull on the first day of the Trek, said: 'You've done what Super League couldn't do. You've merged Widnes and Warrington.' That was the original plan, of course, that the two clubs, in return for the big wad of money from

News Ltd., would submerge their cherished identities in a new joint venture. On the day they voted at an interminable meeting at Wigan to accept that blueprint, I came out of Central Park to find Peter Higham and the then Widnes chairman, the formidable Jim Mills, deep in conversation. 'Working out the merger?' I asked them naively.

They both gave me the look reserved for those terminally wet behind the ears. 'We're not merging,' they said, like a Greek chorus.

'But you've just voted for it.'

'We've voted for the money. Now we're working out how to get out of the merger.'

XII

Widnes: Homeward Bound

PAUL SIMON WROTE 'HOMEWARD BOUND' ON WIDNES RAILWAY
station. There was a plaque there to prove it the last time I looked. He
was on one of his early '60s, pre-Garkunkel forays to England at the
time, learning his trade by doing floor-spots in rooms above shabby
pubs. I saw him doing just that in Bury and wouldn't have advised him
to give up his day job. He has written a lot of better songs in the course
of selling millions of records since, but the one he wrote in Widnes still
stands up as a rather touching evocation of homesickness. And if there
was ever a town to make you feel wistful for wherever it is you come
from, be it Manhattan or Runcorn, this is it. It is not a place which
makes the heart rise in anticipation as you approach it, even knowing
that it marks the end of 220 miles of unaccustomed effort and even in
such distinguished company as the Widnes coach, Neil Kelly, and Ken,
the dyslexic architect, who is back with us for the big finish.

Neil, an import from Wakefield via Dewsbury, is particularly
interested in the route we took through West Yorkshire. 'Ah yes, I
signed so-and-so there,' he says at one juncture, naming one of his
pre-season recruits. 'Should have left him there.'

The outside world's image of the town we are approaching is
perhaps best summed up by an advertising campaign with which
Warrington promoted the Super League match between the two
clubs a few weeks later – the last ever to be played at Wilderspool,

apart from a friendly at Christmas and maybe just one or two others. It featured a graphic representation of Widnes as a polluted wasteland, complete with leaking chemical drums and a three-eyed fish. Widnes put in an official complaint, but Warrington – unlike Halifax, who were fined for referring to Bradford fans as 'retards' in their match programme – escaped punishment. Friendly local rivalry, where would we be without it?

There was a time when Widnes could not have sued anyone for labelling it as a toxic dump, because nowhere in the north of England came closer to being rendered uninhabitable by its local industry. J. Fenwick Allen writes that 'Widnes was transformed from a pretty, sunny riverside hamlet, with quiet sleepy ways, into a settlement of thousands of labouring men, unfinished streets and works belching forth volumes of the most deleterious gases and clouds of black smoke.' I can think of a few players, including one or two signed by Neil, who have perpetuated those sleepy ways, but I'd like to have seen that 'pretty, sunny riverside hamlet'. All trace of it was obliterated by the alkali industry which was established in Widnes in the mid-nineteenth century. All the raw materials were handy: salt from Cheshire; coal from St Helens; limestone from Derbyshire; sulphur via Liverpool docks. Put them all together and what have you got? The smelliest town in Britain, that's what. Not only did the process itself stink, it also left behind unlimited quantities of a noxious waste product called galligu. According to Arthur Townsend in *The Founding of the Widnes Chemical Industry*, it was 'a putty-like material . . . dumped on the ground in vast heaps, which emitted toxic and flammable gases . . . Another serious pollutant was hydrogen chloride gas which spread across the landscape devastating crops, property and livestock and constituting a health hazard to people living in the vicinity.' The boffins of the time thought they had got around that one by dissolving the gas in water and pumping it into the sewers and rivers as hydrochloric acid, thus seeing off even the three-eyed fish. It's all different now. Widnes still has its chemical works, but they now produce dainty, bijou quantities of boutique chemicals and don't even smell. They are, Mr Townsend writes, 'speciality chemicals, often of great complexity and value, sold in relatively small quantities for sophisticated applications'. Posh stuff. Widnes now, inevitably, has its museum devoted to the choking glory days of the chemical industry – Catalyst – built next to Spike Island, where many of the early works were set up. In those days, you could bring anyone with a working knowledge of the north of England to the place in a blindfold and ask them where they were.

'Widnes,' they would reply unerringly, if they had any sense of smell at all. 'Somewhere between Waterloo Road and Ditton Road.'

Paul Simon no doubt got a good nostril-full of it all in the early '60s, although he doesn't mention it as one of his reasons for wanting to get back to New York at the earliest possible opportunity. He does, however, sing:

> Sitting in the railway station
> Got a ticket for my destination,

which implies that Widnes had a booking office in those days. It's amazing the things you can learn from old songs.

That railway station is set in the perfectly agreeable suburbs to the north of the town centre – a town centre which, along with the lingering stench of the chemicals that gave the Chemics their name, gives the place its less than glowing reputation. There was that story about the Widnesian who went on a TV quiz show.

'And where are you from, sir?' he was asked.

'Widnes.'

'I'm sorry.'

'I said I'm from Widnes.'

'I heard you. I'm just sorry.'

Widnes could yet have the last laugh. A recent survey revealed that house prices were rising faster there than anywhere in the country, with the average shooting up from £95,000 to £155,000 in a mere blink of an eye. People are not flocking to the town because of its vibrant, cosmopolitan atmosphere, however. What little it has to offer is split into several segments by dual carriageways, but, if you put it all together, it would still make Castleford really look like Las Vegas and St Helens like the best bits of New York, Rome and Paris all rolled into one. Of all the towns in which rugby league is played, it has always seemed to me to be the most soul-destroying.

Bearing left after the power station, we come to Simms Cross, home of one of the most famous amateur clubs around these parts – they progressed as far as playing Wigan in the Challenge Cup in 2003 – and, judging by the signboard above the pub doorway, once the site of an actual cross that gave it the name. The name of its club has undergone a transformation that has affected a number of institutions in the town, because it is now known officially as Halton Simms Cross, after the borough formed by the amalgamation of Widnes and its neighbour across the Mersey, Runcorn. Widnes now play at the Halton Stadium, rebuilt on the site of Naughton Park, which is also home to Runcorn FC, who also have a Halton tagged on somewhere or other. You would have to live halfway across the bridge between the two to regard yourself as a native of Halton; otherwise you come from either Widnes or Runcorn.

If you come from Widnes, you know all about Jim Mills, the fearsome Welshman who 'Came North' from Cardiff to sign for Halifax in 1964, but who carved out most of his career and his home on the banks of the Mersey. Big Jim, as it is reckoned to be wise to call him, was sent off 15 times in his British rugby league career, along with various diplomatic incidents elsewhere in the world, including being effectively banned from New Zealand. You can only speak as you find, though, and, on the one occasion I played against him, he was a considerate, even a gentlemanly opponent. He didn't know me from Adam that night when Blackpool Borough A team came to Naughton Park and found themselves a man short. For all he knew, I could have been a young hot-head, intent on making a name for himself. He made his point about how ill-advised this would be by taking me firmly by the collar at the first scrum and lifting me one-armed up into the air with these words: 'Let's keep it nice and steady, shall we?' I felt it was a reasonable proposition, concisely put, and we kept it nice and steady.

They say that Jim has equally little trouble keeping order at his nightclub, which is on our way into town. As we approach, the door is ajar and we think that he might just be inside, clearing up after the previous night's excesses, disposing of the bodies of any customers who caused any problems. We give him a shout, but instead summon up the equally imposing figure of Esene Faimalo, a formidable Kiwi forward in Doug Laughton's teams of the late '80s and early '90s. That surely has to be the definition of a successful nightclub: when you need Esene Faimalo on the door at 11.30 in the morning.

As we walk, I find my opinion of Widnes town centre improving; mind you, I've never been through it before at the head of a couple of hundred people, some of them beating drums and chanting insults to all things Widnesian. Despite that, the town is unmistakably wearing a smile; the sun is shining, people are sitting at kerbside cafés, sipping cappuccinos. I'm beginning to see what Terry O'Connor means about Widnes looking beautiful. We sweep down Milton Road, ignoring the short cut I normally take through the bowling club, turn right into Lowerhouse Lane and there we are. There isn't exactly a brass band playing, but there easily could be. Ken is wearing a self-designed T-shirt reading 'We Did It!'. Well, we think he did it, but there's no way of really being sure. Others had less luck with their apparel. Some idea of the sort of unbridled event it was can be gleaned from the following heart-rending letter, which appeared in *League Express* the following week:

Would Vikings fans please keep a lookout for a cruel thief who struck last Friday afternoon?

Last week my girlfriend bought me a Vikings' home jersey and seven pairs of Widnes underpants, each with a day of the week printed on the backside. After washing them on Friday morning, I left them out to dry and wandered up town to cheer on Stevo and Clarkey and to hand over a cheque from our pub dominoes team, of which I am captain.

When I returned, six pairs of underpants and my Widnes shirt had vanished off the washing line.

Although I don't expect anyone to find my briefs, someone may spot my Widnes top as it is unique and has the number nine on the back and my nickname 'SKINMAN' emblazoned on the back as well. If anyone is seen wearing it who isn't 6 ft 2 in. with grey hair, he is probably the thief.

Jamie Porteous, Widnes.

At least they didn't steal the pair which he was, presumably, wearing; it wasn't quite as wild an affair as that. I hope he benefited, by way of compensation, from the share-out of surplus rations from the campervan. There are probably still people in Widnes living on energy drinks and slightly curly Tesco tuna and sweetcorn sandwiches. Apart from the feeding of the 5,000 – well maybe 500 – the arrival was soon to have other religious undertones. As a staunch Catholic, Phil slipped effortlessly into Papal mode and took the rest of us with him. Down we dropped onto our creaking knees in Widnes' car park and kissed the tarmac. It's astonishing what a combination of sun, exhaustion, TV cameras and maybe, just maybe, a few residual chemical fumes will make you do. The tarmac had a slightly puttyish consistency and a bit of a funny flavour. It reminded me of something I couldn't quite put a name to. That's it – galligu! And don't it taste good.

* * *

And that's it, really. Except that it doesn't feel anything like the far extremity of Rugby League Land. You can't stand in Widnes' car park and persuade yourself that you're staring into the void, with nothing but unknown dangers and pagan ways beyond. You have to go a little deeper into Widnes for that. You have to go to West Bank.

West Bank is the bit of Widnes beyond Spike Island and the remnants of the chemical industry. It is not to be confused with the Palestinian enclave of the same name beyond the River Jordan, although in the old days, with the wind blowing in the wrong direction, it could have been equally uncongenial. It must have been a bit like being under attack from some shadowy paramilitary organisation – Provisional ICI, perhaps. The day I approached it, on the other hand, there was a hint of the sunny, riverside hamlet that used to be here, complete with the maritime equivalent of a car-boot sale at the marina where the St Helens Canal meets the Mersey. With the railway here as well, this was the world's first transport interchange. Make a note of this; it could be the last 'first' of the trip.

As you come around the nose of the promontory sticking out into the river, you find yourself on a promenade, built to commemorate

Queen Victoria's 60th Jubilee. It sounds as unlikely a proposition as Wigan Pier, but Widnes Prom has never quite achieved the same music-hall notoriety. It's the real thing, though, designed for strolling along in the evening amid the bracing fumes, even if the only people on it that day were a couple of local youths, stripped to the waist and drinking cans of lager, whilst they tormented a younger lad who had been left in their charge. There is even what looks, at first sight, like a refreshment kiosk, but which turns out, on closer inspection, to be the northern terminus of the old transporter bridge, which replaced the Runcorn Ferry – immortalised in one of Stanley Holloway's monologues – and was replaced itself in 1961 by the present Runcorn Bridge. Now this, from the right angle, is a real shock to the eye – especially if you happen to be one of the numerous Australians who have come to Widnes over the years to play rugby league – because, apart from Sydney's structurally irrelevant stone towers, it is a more or less exact two-thirds scale model of the Sydney Harbour Bridge. Its arch rises above West Bank, the way that Sydney's does above The Rocks. Homesick Aussies might get a second jolt if they visit when the tide is out, because then the Mersey can be transformed into an expanse of golden sands, stretching all the way to Runcorn. OK, as a view it might not quite rank with Sydney Harbour or Bondi Beach, but it's a lot more unexpected – another example, of which there have been many across Rugby League Land, of the capacity of places you think you know to surprise you. Across the sands, in its channel running along the Runcorn bank, there is the Manchester Ship Canal. On certain days of the year, you can catch a Mersey Ferry from the spruced-up Salford Quays, all the way to the Pier Head in Liverpool, passing a strange mixture of industrial desolation and defiant patches of greenery; a village built by Italian prisoners-of-war; and salt-marsh islands used to graze animals. I did the trip with, amongst others, the senior referee, Steve Ganson, one summer day. It's normally non-stop from Salford to Liverpool, but on this occasion we tied up briefly near Warrington, because Steve had sent a couple off, just after he had himself been warned for back-chat by two lady pensioners in the bar. In Runcorn you go past the old football ground, also home at one time to Runcorn Highfield, who, unlike Simms Cross, went on strike rather than play Wigan in the Cup. From that vantage point, Widnes, with its soaring bridge – and even I won't try to kid you that it was Paul Simon's inspiration for 'Bridge Over Troubled Water' – and its promenade, looks rather grand. So must have been the Mersey Hotel, in its shadow, when it was in its heyday. People must have come here for a day out, using its now-neglected bowling greens and gardens. You can still get a Sunday lunch for £2.50 and it is the aroma of gravy, rather than anything more sinister, which floats on the air in West Bank. Inside, there is one of the long, framed photos of touring teams you see on the walls of pubs throughout Rugby League Land, in this case the 1992 side, including three Widnes players, and you can buy a ticket for the Widnes Amateur Rugby League Draw. It feels like the last outpost of rugby league as the dominant sporting culture; beyond here, you might as well be in Liverpool.

* * *

Back at what was once Naughton Park – named after the one-time club secretary, Tom Naughton – there is a match against Castleford with which to round off the whole thing. Widnes is a rugby league town reborn over the last couple of years, since it got into Super League. It was, of course, a power in the land under the old regime, which, given its modest population of 54,000, is as remarkable a display of overachievement as Featherstone's. Like theirs, it was built on making maximum use of local resources. Their 1934 Challenge Cup final side, beaten by Hunslet, was unique in that every player in it was born in Widnes. The side that won it four years earlier consisted of 12 born-and-bred Widnesians and one South African, whilst the one that carried off the trophy in 1937 was positively cosmopolitan, with 12 players from Widnes and one travelling all the way from Runcorn. How on earth did he make himself understood at training?

Widnes teams of a later vintage tended to be rather more exotic, with a particular liking for scary New Zealanders – like another local nightclub owner who had little trouble from punters, Kurt Sorensen – and Welshmen. One of the familiar sights at the old Naughton Park was the lines of coaches parked outside with places of origin you couldn't hope to pronounce correctly, but in which the letters L and W were performing well beyond the call of duty. They were there to watch the likes of John Devereux, Paul Moriarty and – especially – Jonathan Davies and they were the tip of an iceberg of out-of-town support for a small-town club. Their reputation as the Cup kings and the unmistakable whiff of glamour about them, even before players like that were recruited, meant that people with nothing to do with the place came to Widnes to see them. They must have had a bit of a shock when they arrived. Naughton Park was a dump, with hardly a good view of the action from anywhere. When you go to the Halton Stadium now, you think that, whilst it might not be perfect, this is the ground Widnes should have had when they had a great side. That great side collapsed in an avalanche of debt, which almost put the club out of business and, having made sure there was to be no merger with Warrington, also made sure they missed the cut for Super League. If that competition was the closed shop some of its members would like it to be, that would have been the end for Widnes as a major force in the game. Instead, they have reinvented themselves as a club that can make a go of it in the twenty-first century. Even the old committee – they were the last club to be run by one – has gone, although Neil Kelly is one of those who believe that the board of directors which has replaced it – and of which Jim Mills was once chairman – is itself too unwieldy. They now have a decent support base again, something underlined by the turn-out for our biggest question-and-answer session – and final explanation of the momentum rule – of the whole trip. They now have modern stands on three sides of the ground, with just a stretch of the old, low-rise terracing behind the set of sticks at the Fiddler's Ferry power station end as a reminder of what Naughton Park used to be like.

We have a little charade to go through here, emerging from the players' tunnel to breast a tape on the pitch and officially mark the end of the Trek. Anyone who knew what time we had left Warrington that morning might calculate that it had taken us ten hours to walk the ten miles or so to Widnes – slow progress even for me, even for Ken, even for the drummers. I call it a little charade; in fact, those last few yards were starting to feel like the hardest of the lot. It's all right for Phil and Stevo. They've come out of tunnels like this for major finals, for World Cup finals even; they have no excuse for being nervous. My experience has been rather different – more a matter of slinking apologetically onto muddy fields in the middle of nowhere, with the proverbial three men and a dog asking 'Who's the old bugger with the beard?' I've never heard the dog actually asking that, but I know that's what he's thinking. Even that appearance on the same pitch, a quarter of a century before, had been essentially in private. Now, there are thousands of people out there, waiting impatiently for their chance to hoot and jeer. Small wonder that my motley rugby league life, and in particular the last two weeks of it, was passing before my eyes.

There was that first game I played as a kid, when someone a couple of years older butted me and cut his head open. All the knock-ons with the line open, every missed tackle, the occasional good run or ball slipped out satisfactorily. The old teammates, some I still speak to every week, some I haven't seen for years, one or two dead. The dawning realisation in Blackpool that this wasn't just an adolescent crush, but the real thing, a love affair that was going to dominate my life – a frustrated, thwarted, unrequited love at times, but love just the same. The thousands of games watched from press boxes and touchlines. The stories I should have written and didn't, or the ones I wished I'd done differently or left alone. The places rugby league has taken me. Some of the little tricks and rather bigger deceptions it had taken to get me there. The rough democracy of the game; the way that just about everybody is on first-name terms with everybody else, even if they're knifing them in the back. The times you despair of it and know for a fact that it is going nowhere, except down the tubes fast. The sure and certain knowledge that, if it was, I was going with it. The times when the rest of the world seemed mad and only rugby league truly sane. And still it isn't time to face the baying mob, because the Sky floor manager is saying '30 seconds'.

What is it anyway about this game that makes it so irreplaceable once it enters the bloodstream? Why this senseless yearning for one more game? Why will nothing else do? Stripped down to its fundamentals, I think it's something like this: two men – equal size, ability, commitment – are running towards each other, destined for a collision that is not calculated to do either of them any good. The whole thrust of Western civilisation is that there should be some way of them negotiating themselves out of this collision, but they can't. They have an unspoken contract that it must take place; the only thing at issue is what sort of collision it will be. If they both do it right, they will both get up and be involved in similar collisions a couple of dozen more times in the match, all equally counter-intuitive. You add on all the skill and tactical refinement afterwards, but these are the bare bones and they make every other game look puny by comparison. These are thoughts which have taken up some time, because we are now being told that we are on in 30 seconds.

So I turned my mind to the last fortnight. That elusive feeling of all being in it together, us and just about everyone we met – apart from that bloke in Leigh. The sun shining on the Humber and the Pennines; the rain tippling down in Bradford and the wind howling through Oldham. The milling city centres; the lonely stretches, with only us on the horizon. The camaraderie that you can only get on a journey; the contributions of Nina, Adam and Marie, Irish Phil and Gill, Uncle Bernard and Andy, Peter and Roy. And Stevo and Phil, of course; talk about chalk and cheese. People have asked me since what it was like spending two weeks with no escape from Stevo – who shares a name, incidentally, with one of the main men in one of my son's favourite TV shows, *Jackass*, which is largely devoted to self-mutilation and the lighting of farts. Mere coincidence? I hardly think so. Is he as loud and brash and bombastic as he is on screen, they ask, obviously expecting me to say that, on the contrary, he is quiet, reflective and self-effacing. No, I say, he's nothing like he is on TV. He's far, far worse. He does have a sensitive side, of course. When a new member of the team joined us in mid-Trek, Stevo greeted him warmly. 'Are you gay?' he bellowed. 'You look like you could be gay.' It's a gift he shared with the Queen Mother, this ability to put people at their ease.

Phil is a different kettle of fish. It has been said of him that he is the hardest man in rugby league to dislodge from a fence once he has got himself comfortably settled onto one. In particular, he is loath to criticise players and will go to great lengths to avoid doing so. I remember once asking him about a former teammate of his at the Sydney Roosters who was coming to play for a British club.

'You'll like him,' he said. 'He's a really good bloke.'

'What's he like as a player?'

'He's a really, really good bloke.'

'Can he play at all?'

'He really is one of the best blokes you'll ever meet.'

'So he can't even play a little bit?'

'He's the most outstandingly good bloke in the history of rugby league.'

And, do you know what? He wasn't much of a player. But what a good bloke!

But there's no more time for such reflections. The Widnes mascot, a little chap in a Viking costume whose idea of pre-match entertainment is to drop his shorts and display to the crowd his fabric bum, is motioning us forward. Bob Connolly, the referee, looks like he wants to check our boots. The Sky floor manager has been saying '30 seconds!' for the last ten minutes. Andy Whitelam is gesticulating wildly. There are cameras up our noses. It's time to try those final few yards. We step out into the floodlit void. There's a roar that suggests one of two possibilities. Either this is quite a popular enterprise or Kemik the Viking has shown his arse again.

XIII

Out on a Limb: London and Cumbria

AND THERE IT REALLY SHOULD END. BUT THERE ARE TWO other places you have to go to if you are to have anything like a rounded picture of professional rugby league in this country, or that, at least, was what I told myself. For separate and distinct ideological reasons, they both have to be included.

Plan A had been for the Trek to start at the London Broncos' ground at Brentford. The party would then walk to King's Cross Station and catch the train to Hull, although one or two people on Humberside made the flattering observation that we were looking quite fresh after walking overnight from the metropolis. We didn't like to tell them that the plan had been abandoned on police insistence; there was no safe walking route that they could sanction between Griffin Park and King's Cross. On a bad day, there's no good way of doing it by car, bus, train or tube either, although for £30 or so a cheery cabbie will let you sit in his stationary taxi for a couple of hours. That tells you all you need to know about London.

In theory, you could walk straight down the A4, the Great West Road, into the middle of London, or possibly skirt around on the North Circular before attacking King's Cross from the blind-side, but you wouldn't seriously expect to survive either experience. Yet people pay incredible amounts of money to live right on these roads and breathe pure lead – and then take the piss out of Northerners and our living arrangements. Give me the middle of the M62 any day.

The impossibility of getting from place to place in London has bedevilled the history of professional rugby league in the city. Sure, there are thousands of exiled Northerners, expatriate Aussies and Kiwis and slowly growing numbers of involved and interested Londoners scattered around the place, but you try persuading them to go to Barnet or Chiswick on a Sunday afternoon, or to anywhere at all on a Friday night. Even some of the London clubs' less obviously off-the-beaten-track locations have raised problems of their own. I remember the Broncos battling to persuade potential fans that, just because Charlton wasn't on the tube map, it wasn't off the edge of the earth. There was a BR station almost next door to The Valley, they said. Indeed there was, and it was conveniently closed on the day they played their first match there. I also recall arriving for one night match at The Stoop to find most of my colleagues frazzled and fraught, with that unmistakable haunted look of those who have either driven through London or wrestled with its public transport. By comparison, I was fresh, fit and raring to go. How had I got there in such mint condition? I'd walked – along the Thames from Tower Bridge. It had taken seven hours, with one or two refreshment stops, but it had been stress-free and I had seen a colony of parrots in a tree on the riverbank at Kew.

I have tended to judge rugby league venues in London by their proximity, or usually otherwise, to Tower Bridge, because for 20-odd years that was where my mate Dave – one of that legion of Daves previously mentioned – had his flat. He should have had a grant from the Sports Council, because for every rugby league event in the capital just about every square inch of the flat would be occupied by someone sleeping it off. He even used the attic above the next-door flat as an extra bedroom. They thought they had rats; in fact, they had Wigan fans. It was into one of his previous flats in East Finchley that we once crammed 56 overnight guests after the 1971 Cup final – Leigh 24 Leeds 7, lest we forget – but Tower Hill came close to that crowd record on a couple of occasions. Somewhere in Wigan, there is still a framed bill from a trendy local restaurant on one Wembley trip in the mid-'80s, which is produced with a flourish on high holidays and feast days like a holy relic that proves the miraculous expensiveness of London. The restaurant specialised in pies – not meat and potato, but venison and wild mushroom, chorizo and rocket, that sort of thing. The bill doesn't record that. It simply states: '4 Pies – £16'.

That flat was the base for too many Cup finals, internationals and assorted club matches to count, including, in recent years, visits to unlikely places like the London Skolars on White Hart Lane or the South London Storm at Thornton Heath. It is now possible to say, for the first time in rugby league's involvement with the capital, that you can play and watch the game there at every level and become hopelessly lost in just about every corner of the city. There are those, 200 miles north, who believe that this doesn't matter, that the Broncos' failure to draw five-figure gates is evidence of the truth of what they have always said – that league will never catch on in London. Was it the Chinese leader, Chou En-lai, who when asked his opinion of the success of the French Revolution replied that it was too soon to judge? If he did, he might have said the same about rugby league in London; you wouldn't fully appreciate the importance of it until it was gone. One thing I do know is that, if you took the Broncos out of the equation, the level of interest in the sport in national newspaper offices in and around Canary Wharf would plunge like a computer being thrown out of a 28th-floor window.

Meanwhile, sadly, the flat has been sold. Dave has married a lady who refers to the North as 'the frozen' and has moved to Marlow. He has done his best to round up all the various sets of keys from all the temporary residents over the years, but one night the Singaporean businessman who has bought it is going to come in from a hard day's wheeling and dealing and find a couple of Doncaster supporters curled up on his settee, a bloke from Brisbane in his bath and Wiganers in his roof-space.

* * *

If there is a better way of getting to a Broncos match than walking along the Thames towpath, it has to be travelling by limousine from the St Helens Hilton. By dint of some inconsiderate fixture planning, the second week of the Trek was interrupted by London playing Bradford at Griffin Park. We were all supposed to be there and a fast, chauffeur-driven car from 'the frozen' was the obvious answer. I hadn't realised that, if you have a car big and expensive enough, you get a motorway lane to yourself, in the manner of Politburo members in the good old days in Moscow. Nor had I appreciated that Birmingham can look quite habitable if you swish past swiftly and view it through tinted windows. We pass the time with one of Stevo's more memorable stories, about the time he accepted the job of London coach and was all set to leave for the airport and fly over from Sydney when a club functionary phoned up to abuse him. He unpacked his suitcase, decided to stick with his television work and the rest is history.

And so it was that, only a matter of moments after leaving St Helens, we were being waved into the Sky compound at Griffin Park. For my money, it is the most congenial home rugby league has had in London since Craven Cottage. Apart from an ageing cockney wide-boy on the gate who tells people 'Yer want ter get dahn ter Twickers. That's yer proper rugby, innit?' you could be making your way into one of the older northern rugby league grounds. It even has the perfect symmetry of a pub on each corner, although which is serving a decent pint of London Pride at any given time is a closely guarded secret. More than anywhere on the northern circuit, however, there is the feeling at Brentford of a social gathering, of people from disparate lifestyles in different parts of the city's huge sprawl all converging for a purpose. On this particular night, I see people I know from the Skolars and the Storm and old mates of Dave's from the London League. Just about everyone has had to make an effort, be it the just mildly gruelling feat of getting here from Ealing a couple of miles away or the Labour of Hercules involved in crossing the whole metropolis, if you happen to be a convert from Charlton or Greenwich who is keeping the faith. Griffin Park is short of fancy entertainment facilities, but it has something better – a compact area behind the stand that is just the right size for spectators, players and everyone else to hang around and have a beer after the match, before diving off in one direction of the compass or other to one of the quartet of pubs. It's a sociable set-up.

It's a good place to watch a game as well, with its assortment of wooden stands, tight to the touchline, even if they aren't exactly full. This is where it becomes slightly more difficult to wax enthusiastic about the Broncos. On a beautiful summer night, just eight days after their first win of the season at Griffin Park, with the Super League favourites and eventual champions in town and a place of their own in the play-offs to go for, there were 3,651 in the ground. There were probably a couple of thousand others on the way, stuck in traffic jams on the Hanger Lane gyratory or sweltering in broken-down trains on the Piccadilly line. It isn't the rugby league club that doesn't work – although their defence was not at its best in a dismal 60–6 defeat – it's the city.

Having stocked up with exotic bottled beers and upmarket thirst-inducing snacks, the trip back to St Helens flashes past even more quickly. I'm sure I was tucked up in the St Helens Hilton earlier than I would have been back at Tower Bridge. Perhaps that is the answer. If Rupert Murdoch wants the London element of the competition he invested in to be a success, he needs to provide a fleet of stretch limos, and possibly the private toll roads to accommodate them, to criss-cross the capital on match-days. It's worth a try before we kick it into that infinitely capacious rugby league receptacle – the too-hard basket.

* * *

There is another part of England that has been shoved into that basket – an area which many people in the game would argue deserves to have more emphasis put on it than London. John Monie, often a fount of wisdom on all matters rugby league, once argued that we would be better off putting our effort and money there – which was an interesting viewpoint, considering that he was the London coach at the time. It is Cumbria.

We were never going to be walking anywhere near there, but, like someone with a bad conscience about not visiting an elderly and ailing relative, I knew I had a duty to go there for this book, whether they were going to contribute much to the conversation or not.

Cumbria is important for all the opposite reasons to London. It is remote, underpopulated and historically attached to the sport. It has long-established amateur clubs like Ellenborough and Egremont, to name two who have taken professional scalps in the recent past, and a record of producing an abundance of players. But, like London, we ignore it at our peril.

It is also a bit of an odd geographical construct, combining the old counties of Cumberland and Westmorland with a big chunk of Lancashire. That Lancastrian outpost, which included places like Barrow and Ulverston, makes little sense when you look at an atlas now. It doesn't even share a land border with the rest of the county. It's only when you consider that a stagecoach across the sands of Morecambe Bay was the best transport option that it begins to look connected to Lancaster, Preston and the rest of the world.

When Barrow was in Lancashire it was a positive powerhouse of the game, with the money made from shipbuilding helping to finance daring transfer raids on the vulnerable South, on clubs like Wigan and St Helens, to bring in imports to play alongside local talent of the calibre of Willie Horne. They were sometimes known as the Millionaires, which takes a bit of crediting now, when you wander around a town that has lost its *raison d'être* with the closure of the shipyards. There is nowhere in the north of England – except possibly Spurn Point on the opposite coast – that feels more like the ends of the earth than Walney Island. When one Tongan forward was out for a training run on the beach there, he was arrested as a suspected illegal immigrant. The mystery is where they thought he might have arrived from, because you drop off the globe a couple of miles to the west.

Barrow, known for their raids in their moneybags era, are now officially known as the Raiders. The reason for this odd state of affairs is that they were merged some years ago with the team then known as Carlisle Border Raiders, from 50 miles away at the other end of the county. It was a back-door way of getting shut of Carlisle, whose Border Raiders tag was bizarrely transferred to Barrow, with the implication that they were about to start pillaging over the Lancashire boundary in Carnforth.

Carlisle was left to fend for itself, although, at the time of writing, it looked as though their successful team in the Rugby League

Conference, the summer competition intended for clubs outside the mainstream, might be stepping onwards and upwards into the National League structure. Full marks for resilience if they make it, because they were left out on the mountain to die, the way in which rugby league has traditionally disposed of its sickly offspring.

Talking of which, Super League started with a Cumbrian representative – and that experience almost killed them. Workington Town won just two games, finished two points adrift of Paris St Germain at the foot of the table and averaged just 2,322 at their home games. The following season, they finished bottom of the First Division, with fewer than 1,600 a time watching their matches. The next year, they were next to bottom of Division Two, averaging little more than 800. So when people say that what Super League needs is a club in Cumbria, then the sceptical response is that when they had one it was hardly a resounding success and that Town have been struggling to recover from being in Super League ever since.

Part of the problem is that Workington is a small town and it cannot realistically hope to draw spectators from its neighbour a mere seven miles away. I was once shown the patch of ground halfway between Workington and Whitehaven that was earmarked for their post-merger stadium, but the only thing less likely than that merger is that Whitehaven people will go to watch a Workington team in Super League, or vice versa. Harry Edgar, the founder of *Open Rugby*, tells me that, in his youth, he would go on the train from Whitehaven with his dad to watch glamorous Barrow, but that is not quite the same as watching the Jam-eaters.

Ah, yes, Jam-eaters. This trawl through Rugby League Land has been liberally sprinkled with the names, like codheads and pie-eaters, that natives of one town call natives of the next, but this is one of the most intriguing. It is a fair bet that the miners of both towns – and this is an area where the thesis that coal equals rugby league stands up unassisted – ate their fair share of jam and bread, but neither like to admit it. One version says that they did so in order to get the coal dust out of their throats. The local broadcaster, John Cox, has a different variant, in which Cornishmen imported to work the iron ore mines between the two towns were paid more than the local rate and could afford the luxury of jam on their bread to moisten their dry mouths while underground in the pits. To residents of each town, the other mob are the aliens, the Jam-eaters. It recalls the importance of the right terminology in other contexts: 'He is a terrorist. You are a guerrilla. I am a freedom-fighter.' In West Cumbria, it goes: 'He is a Jam-eater. You are a Cumbrian. I am a Marrer.'

For me, opportunities to mix with the Marrers have been limited in recent years, since the precipitous decline of Workington and the disappearance of the Cumbrian county side. The only chances have been the occasional Cup tie and the odd Russian tour game, so when I learned that, a couple of months after the end of the Trek and a day after the Super League Grand Final, Cumbria were to play as an entity for the first time in nine years, wild horses would not have kept me away from the Recreation Ground in Whitehaven.

* * *

The only way to go to a match in Cumbria is the way that visiting fans have traditionally done it, by making a day of it. Some head for the obvious tourist spots en route. Cumbria signifies one thing to the outside world and that is lakes, which means that a little gem of a town like Cockermouth, a few miles beyond Bassenthwaite and the birthplace of that Lakeland icon, William Wordsworth, is largely left to its own devices. An even bigger surprise to the unwary visitor is Whitehaven itself. The first impression, as you come past the Pelican Garage that traditionally marks the point beyond which 'Haven's home form deserts them, is of a run-down coastal mining town, but there is a lot more to it than that. In the mid-eighteenth century, Whitehaven was the second-busiest port in the country, not far behind London and leaving pretenders like Liverpool, Bristol and Newcastle far behind in its wake. The importing of rum, tea and tobacco had something to do with it, as did a spot of dabbling in the slave trade, but the bulk of the traffic consisted of Cumbrian coal destined for Ireland. This was an important place, especially if you were Irish and cold.

Until recently, those halcyon days took a lot of imagining, but now that the harbour has been restored it is possible to visualise the bustle and energy of those times. It is also easier now to picture the scene when the American captain, John Paul Jones, a Scot who had learnt his maritime skills sailing out of Whitehaven, sailed back in and tried to make his contribution to the War of Independence by setting fire to the fleet moored there. The way Daniel Hay describes it in *Whitehaven: A Short History*, it was a fairly chaotic enterprise, with a number of Jones' subordinates feigning illness to avoid getting involved and the townspeople chasing the Americans away after they had only slightly damaged a couple of ships. Far more serious was the tally of over 70 of the port's vessels captured or sunk by them or the French during the war.

Back from the harbour, Whitehaven is full of buildings from its Georgian and Victorian heydays, some of them recycled for uses which could hardly have been envisaged. The classically styled tearooms, built in 1856, are now the Chattanooga Kebab and Pizza House. The lady at The Beacon, the new museum overlooking the harbour, says that it was the fact that Whitehaven was not considered worth redeveloping in the 1960s that saved it. These days, it might be the towns and villages of the Lakes that are overrun by Japanese tourists, but it is Whitehaven and Cockermouth that have been designated as Gem Towns, because of their unspoilt architectural heritage.

From either The Beacon or the quays that thrust out into the Irish Sea beyond it, you can look up and down the Cumbrian coast. Just south of the harbour is the Candlestick Chimney which marks the remains of the Wellington Pit, in which 136 men and boys died in the area's worst mining disaster in 1910. Tunnels from Cumbrian pits went miles out under the sea, which meant that their disasters tended to be bad ones. The last shaft mine, the Haig, closed in 1987 and the area's biggest employer, by some distance, is Sellafield power station – aka Smiling Sands – another dozen miles down the coast.

The cliffs to the north of the town are the spectacular setting for a number of junior rugby league grounds. I went to one of the lesser-known ones in the mid-'90s, when a works team called Smith Brothers – paper manufacturers, who had taken over the Cumberland Curled Hair Manufacturing Co. Ltd, Mr Hay tells me – took the momentous decision to switch from rugby union, which was such a minority pursuit that they had no one to play. Their ground was perched yards from the cliff edge, so the obvious question was how many balls they lost in a season. Hardly any, they told me, because the up-draught blowing off the sea carried them back to safety, rather than allowing them to drop onto the rocks hundreds of feet below. They let me try it and, whilst touch-kicking was never my forte, it was exactly as they said; the kick took the ball over the cliff and the wind brought it right back again. It's only right and proper that rugby league should be played there, in such an elemental location.

On the day of the big Cumbria versus New Zealand A match, that indefatigable student of the game, Mike Latham, and I were greatly impressed by the lady in The Beacon instantly deducing that we were there for that purpose. That just shows, we thought, how deeply ingrained in the place rugby league still is. Then we realised that we were wearing identical freebie fleeces, with 'Tetley's Super League' embroidered on them in three-inch high letters and that it wasn't quite the feat of detection that it might have appeared. In Workington, they might have thrown us out.

* * *

As we neared the Recreation Ground, it was clear that something remarkable was happening. Not only were there hundreds, nay thousands, of people on their way to the ground, there were even fans wearing the blue of Workington – who didn't even have a player in the Cumbria side – rather than 'Haven's unique chocolate, blue and gold. That is what I call a good selling job, evidence of the Rugby Football League rolling up its sleeves and promoting the fixture in Whitehaven and beyond. Over 4,000 filed up past the Miners' Welfare Club and into the Recre' – which might not sound too fantastic until you consider how neglected representative rugby in the county has been. It was, without exception, the most uplifting occasion of the year. Local children danced a mass haka, which they had been taught by 'Haven's Kiwi prop, David Fatialofa, and the match was one of unmitigated ferocity and passion, summing up everything that I love about this game. These weren't the best players in the world – they weren't even the best players in

Cumbria, in some cases – but, by God, they meant it. Midway through the match, as they were in the process of building up an inspired 24-point lead, they brought on Paul Davidson, who I had last seen walking through Halifax with us, and who ranks as the most extreme case of an unreconstructed hard-man still extant in the game. His opposite number, one George Tuakura, had a very similar approach to the game, but shouldn't have had a clue about Davidson or his reputation. The way that the two men looked at each other with instant recognition, however, meant that, in the first tackle, they were honour-bound to create old-fashioned mayhem. They did. Mike and I looked at each other and said the same two words: 'Pre-emptive strike.'

In the last 12 minutes, the Kiwis scored four converted tries for a 24-all draw – a storyline you would not attempt if you were making it up. It made for a reasonably happy return to the Cumbrian coast for the New Zealand A coach, Gerard Stokes. He had some experience of playing around these parts, but he was quick to point out what that did and didn't make him. 'I'm not a Jam-eater,' he said, with just a tinge of irritation. 'I'm a Marrer.' Which could mean 'I'm not from Whitehaven. I'm from Workington,' or 'I'm not from Workington. I'm from Whitehaven.' Take your pick. One thing the summer had taught me, though, is that, in some unfathomable way, it matters.

Postscript

THE DAY BEFORE THAT TRIP TO CUMBRIA, PHIL AND STEVO handed over a cheque for more than £54,000 to Outward Bound on the pitch at Old Trafford, at half-time in the Super League Grand Final. They wanted me to help them – well, it was a very big cheque – but I had a ready-made excuse in having to file copy to the *Independent on Sunday*, with the girls in Howden no doubt waiting impatiently for my every word. If I'm being completely honest, there was a deeper reason for me being up in the stand, rather than down on the turf. I had struggled for any sort of composure in front of 5,698 at Widnes when we finished the Trek; to have strutted my stuff in front of 65,537 – the first sell-out for a Grand Final – would have made it not so much the Theatre of Dreams for me as the Theatre of Brown Trousers. Bradford beat Wigan, who had done so well to get there with an unbeaten run under Mike Gregory, in a fairly predictable manner. It was OK, but it wasn't as good as Cumbria versus New Zealand A.

That marked the end of the domestic season, but, after it, two terrible things happened. Great Britain lost the Ashes series 3–0. Nothing too unusual about that, I can hear you say, because we've been losing to Australia since 1970. Where this was different was that we could and should have won all three of those matches against what I still say was a severely sub-standard Kangaroo side.

That nice boy, Adrian Morley, got himself sent off by Steve Ganson for a high tackle after 12 seconds of the first Test (and got nicked for drink-driving in Salford a couple of weeks later). David Waite handled his substitutions – including using Barrie McDermott for just three minutes in that match – in a manner so bizarre that it made that conversation with him in the Gaping Goose seem positively sensible by comparison. In all three games, Great Britain were in a winning position in the last five minutes; in all three, they found a way of losing.

As if that wasn't bad enough, over on the other side of the globe, England were winning the Rugby (Union) World Cup. Now, I hope I've made it clear that I've got nothing against rugby union. Confined to its natural niche in Rugby League Land, played between consenting adults in private, it does no real harm. But by becoming the first home-grown side to win a world championship in a major team sport since Great Britain – with Stevo at hooker – won the Rugby (League) World Cup in 1972, however, they had upped the ante. On the day that they – and Jason Robinson – beat Australia in the final and Great Britain blew it again in the third Test, I was in the Slubbers Arms afterwards – an appropriate venue after something which had been done so imperfectly and carelessly – drinking Taylor's Landlord to forget. Some jokers took the easy option of winding me up with the usual 'union's brilliant, league's a load of crap' business. I should have ignored them. Instead, I took the bait and turned into a raving maniac. I'd like to apologise to everybody in the pub that night. Even worse, the nice lady who lives next door to Mike Latham remarked over the garden fence that he must have been very happy that England had won 'the rugby'. Now, Mike is normally a man so polite and correct that he makes other accountants look like a particularly ill-disciplined chapter of the Hell's Angels, but he ripped into her in a way that necessitated a shamefaced visit to apologise the next day. When the new season starts, I'm fully expecting a new wave of the writers they send up from London every so often to report on the death of rugby league. Whenever I see those familiar faces, I try to remember to greet them with a friendly: 'Bloody hell! I didn't realise we were in that much trouble again.'

The game is in crisis, of course, but it always has been. It's just a question of what particular sort of crisis it is in. If my 220-mile journey across Rugby League Land had taught me anything, though – apart from not to ask Stevo about the momentum rule – it is that the game is surprisingly well adapted to living with crisis. We used to have the problem, unique in sport, of another game doing everything it could to strangle us. Now we have the subtly different challenge of them wanting to use us as their Swiss finishing school, developing talent – especially in the inner cities, where rugby union has no natural feel for the environment – so that it can be cherry-picked by them later. I tried to avoid the Rugby (Union) World Cup final, but it was on in the gym and the sinking feeling I had in the pit of my stomach was due not just to over-exertion on the rowing machine, but also to the suspicion than England's victory was going to shift the balance of power. I know I wasn't alone. 'I tried to be glad for England,' Johnny Vegas – who still hasn't had his quid from *Viz*, but is hoping for an out-of-court settlement – told me, 'because I like us beating Australia at anything. But I've got very mixed feelings about it. There was a bit of me that couldn't whole-heartedly approve. If that sounds like we've got a chip on our shoulders, it's probably because we're entitled to one, after what we had to put up with for years. Even when they became openly professional, instead of just paying boot money, and started to take our best players, it felt like punishment.'

It is not inconceivable that there could be more of that sort of punishment to come, but there is another way of looking at it, one which St Helens were keen on expounding that night on top of the tower in Liverpool. I call it Wimbledon Syndrome. For a couple of weeks after Tim Henman's latest heroic failure, all the public tennis courts in Britain are full of kids. Inevitably, England's victory will achieve the same effect for rugby, but possibly for league as well as union. Kids don't know the difference; if you wandered far from the route of this book, for that matter, you would find plenty of adults who don't know the difference. I take the little club I'm involved with in Bolton as a bit of a barometer of these things. The week after the World Cup, we had an extra ten young players at training, a couple of them in England replica shirts. More significantly, there was one in a Wigan shirt, a fifth columnist who had apparently said to them: 'If you fancy playing a bit of rugby, I know somewhere we can go.' We tried to make it a good night for them, to show them the forbidden joys of running and passing.

So, until the coffin lid is nailed down, I'm going to continue to work on the principle that there will still be people to play rugby league, people to watch it, to read newspaper articles and even to read books about it, otherwise the last 70,000 words have been rather a waste of time. I hope I haven't just painted a picture of a game which is irredeemably barmy, because the times when I believe that rugby league is perfectly rational and it is just the rest of the world that's lost its marbles come more and more frequently. Where league can sometimes seem loopy is that it lives in a state of constant flux. In 2004, for instance, we are ditching the Origin Match – no trip up the Standedge Tunnel, then – and introducing a Tri-Nations tournament involving Australia and New Zealand that looks, to me at least, completely barking and most unlikely to go ahead in its advertised form. It will be shown on Sky, rather than the BBC, as will, after protracted negotiations, Super League games. That means that Stevo will be back, which will clearly be the cue for national rejoicing that will put that World Cup mullarkey into the shade. What else has happened? Ryan Bailey and Chev Walker are out of jail; Leon Pryce never went. Chris Anderson was sacked at Cronulla and Stuart Raper got his job. Warrington are still playing farewell games at Wilderspool and Bradford are threatening to pull the roof down if they don't get their way over the salary cap. Everything changes; everything stays much the same.

I'm glad, though, to have had the opportunity to take a snapshot of the game – or, more specifically, the setting in which it is played – at a moment in time. I will always remember the long haul that it involved with a slight twinge of discomfort in the feet and an extra twist on the thirst ratchet in the throat. At the end of the season, I ran into Johnny Whiteley at Hull. As is his wont, he was full of congratulations and enthusiasm and a hint of regret that he couldn't have done the whole 220 miles himself, as he would no doubt have been well capable of doing. I was destined to disappoint him. 'Johnny,' I said, 'I let you down. Halfway through that third day, I had a little sip of water.' He gave me a look of pity mingled with gentlemanly disdain.

A couple of weeks later, my mate Rob the Roofer – not to be confused with Bob the Builder – returned from a job in a state of high excitement. I had told him of my studies in this field and he had discovered that he had been working in those heathen parts in which they refer to barmcakes as teacakes.

'But, where I come from, teacakes have currants in them,' he told them in the bakers. 'What do I ask for if I want a currant teacake?'

'You ask for a currant teacake.'

We might not have solved a lot of the other major philosophical questions, but that is surely the last word on that subject. It's a lesson I shall try to remember. Don't expect everything to be the same everywhere in Rugby League Land, don't expect the ground-rules to be the same next season as they were last, just relish it – warts, currants and all.